I0003459

Scratch Cookbook

A quick and easy guide for building Scratch programs intended for further learning through projects, such as interactive animations and games

Brandon Milonovich

[PACKT]
PUBLISHING

open source *
community experience distilled

BIRMINGHAM - MUMBAI

Scratch Cookbook

Copyright © 2013 Packt Publishing

All rights reserved. No part of this book may be reproduced, stored in a retrieval system, or transmitted in any form or by any means, without the prior written permission of the publisher, except in the case of brief quotations embedded in critical articles or reviews.

Every effort has been made in the preparation of this book to ensure the accuracy of the information presented. However, the information contained in this book is sold without warranty, either express or implied. Neither the author, nor Packt Publishing, and its dealers and distributors will be held liable for any damages caused or alleged to be caused directly or indirectly by this book.

Packt Publishing has endeavored to provide trademark information about all of the companies and products mentioned in this book by the appropriate use of capitals. However, Packt Publishing cannot guarantee the accuracy of this information.

First published: July 2013

Production Reference: 1170713

Published by Packt Publishing Ltd.
Livery Place
35 Livery Street
Birmingham B3 2PB, UK.

ISBN 978-1-84951-842-0

www.packtpub.com

Cover Image by Sandeep Vaity (sandeep.vaity@yahoo.com)

Credits

Author

Brandon Milonovich

Reviewers

David Busby

Stamati Crook

Andrew Johns

Martina Kabátová

Pedro Neves Rito

Forest Y. Yu

Acquisition Editor

Joanne Fitzpatrick

Commissioning Editor

Llewellyn Rozario

Lead Technical Editor

Anila Vincent

Technical Editors

Shashank Desai

Krishnaveni Haridas

Mausam Kothari

Pushpak Poddar

Rikita Poojari

Amit Ramadas

Project Coordinator

Hardik Patel

Proofreaders

Maria Gould

Paul Hindle

Indexer

Monica Ajmera Mehta

Graphics

Ronak Dhruv

Production Coordinator

Aparna Bhagat

Cover Work

Aparna Bhagat

About the Author

Brandon Milonovich completed his Master's degree in Teaching and Curriculum with emphasis in Mathematics Education in December 2012 at Syracuse University in central New York. Prior to attending Syracuse, Brandon earned his Bachelor's degree in Adolescent Mathematics Education at The College of Saint Rose in Albany, NY. Brandon grew up in upstate New York with an interest in mathematics and computer science at a young age. Brandon has experience of teaching mathematical concepts to students using Scratch in third through fifth grade, as well as experience of teaching mathematics at the middle school, high school, and university level.

It was during Brandon's time at Saint Rose that he began his work with Scratch through an internship program with Computer Science professor Helen Albanese. In coordination with three Albany City School District teachers, Brandon developed an after-school program centered on programming in Scratch for at-risk youth. The program expanded the following year to include a broader age range of students. Now, Brandon works towards making learning Scratch more accessible within the classroom itself, both with traditional methods and flipped classroom-blended learning style concepts, to build the mathematical foundation students need to be successful 21st century learners. Brandon believes in sharing of information as broadly as possible, and so has presented with his colleagues at numerous conferences and workshops on Scratch, and hopes to continue to do so.

For more information on Brandon, or to contact him, visit `http://www.bmilo.com`.

I would like to thank all of those who have helped me along the way in both the process of writing this book, as well as becoming qualified to write it. Special thanks to Helen Albanese for her continued pushing to work more with Scratch and the opportunities she has provided, as well as a thank you to every professor I had at both the undergraduate and graduate level who have guided me along the way. Thanks also to the Albany City School District for opening its classrooms, particularly to Laurie Ellis, Stephen Costello, Alice Florence, and Timothy Fowler. The greatest thanks of all to my family for their constant support, guidance, and help. Without the amazing group of people I've been surrounded by throughout my life, I would have had little chance of success.

About the Reviewers

David Busby has been a Linux system's admin for around 12 years now and almost always being in a varied role over the years be it development, network admin, support, DBA changing onto a day-to-day basis.

Whenever time permits, he contributes to the EPEL packages for OpenStack and generally follows OpenStack's progress as much as possible.

He has an interest in Infosec, and as a result is generally paranoid about security. He is also familiar with Metasploit, sqlmap, john, and oclHashCat, and has also written a few python tools, and experimented in Golang.

He holds a 2nd Dan black belt in Ju-Jitsu and assists with teaching at a local non-profit club. He also helps to teach a computing class for children at a local school, using Raspberry Pi.

Stamati Crook is a professional programmer with his own software house and consultancy on the south coast of England. He has been involved in teaching Scratch to children at local primary schools and also hopes that his own three children will begin to show more interest in creating games rather than just playing them. His wife, Kathy, also uses Scratch daily in her classroom and you can find lesson plans and resources for children, parents, and teachers learning and teaching Scratch at `http://www.redware.com/scratch`.

Andrew Johns has been a web developer since 1999. He became a STEM Ambassador and Code Club volunteer in 2012, teaching Scratch to primary school children. He currently works for London-based design agency, Pretty, as a Technical Lead. This is the first book for which he has acted as a Technical Reviewer.

Martina Kabátová is a teacher and a researcher in the field of Computer Science education. After completing her PHD, she began to work as an Assistant Professor at Comenius University in Bratislava, Faculty of Mathematics, Physics and Informatics, Department of Informatics Education. Among her responsibilities are several university lectures on programming, educational robotics, and research methodology. Currently, she focuses on educational programming (especial for very young children). She is an author of several study materials and many conference papers dealing with various aspects of Computer Science education. In 2013, she co-authored a book *Transforming Schools in Digital Age*, with Prof. Ivan Kalaš, which summarizes the role of digital technology in education. Martina Kabátová also illustrated this book and she is the author of many illustrations for other computer science textbooks, educational software, and MicroWorlds, and for the Slovak Bebras contest for children in informatics.

Pedro Neves Rito has been working as a professional trainer in the area of information technology and communications for more than 16 years, and as a teacher in higher education for the last six years. He has a Master's degree in Multimedia in Education and is currently a student of the Doctoral program in information systems and technologies. He has used Scratch as a tool for an introduction to programming. Lately, he's been exploring physical computing and Scratch, particularly the use of the Arduino, with the perspective of building activities for primary students. This work has been developed with the help of teachers of different levels of education.

He is currently also an assistant professor at Polytechnic Institute of Viseu, at the School of Education, working in the Department of Communication and Art, in the area of Information Technology and Communication. He works with higher education students, particularly in plastic arts and multimedia, and those pursuing primary education courses (future teachers) and also some that are pursuing Master's courses. In addition to being a teacher in these areas, he has supported a few initiatives outside school that are related to the use of Scratch.

He has started some individual projects, including the writing of two books, which is ongoing. In recent years, he has dedicated most of his time to contributions, by publishing and presenting scientific articles at conferences and some other documents to print media.

Forrest Y. Yu is an author of two books on operating systems. He has a wide range of interests and experiences, including desktop applications, web services, LBS, operating systems, cloud computing, and so on. Recently, he has been working with Amazon building the next generation information security platform and tools. He has a blog http://forrestyu.com/ where you can find more information about him.

www.PacktPub.com

Support files, eBooks, discount offers and more

You might want to visit www.PacktPub.com for support files and downloads related to your book.

Did you know that Packt offers eBook versions of every book published, with PDF and ePub files available? You can upgrade to the eBook version at www.PacktPub.com and as a print book customer, you are entitled to a discount on the eBook copy. Get in touch with us at service@packtpub.com for more details.

At www.PacktPub.com, you can also read a collection of free technical articles, sign up for a range of free newsletters and receive exclusive discounts and offers on Packt books and eBooks.

http://PacktLib.PacktPub.com

Do you need instant solutions to your IT questions? PacktLib is Packt's online digital book library. Here, you can access, read and search across Packt's entire library of books.

Why Subscribe?

- ▸ Fully searchable across every book published by Packt
- ▸ Copy and paste, print and bookmark content
- ▸ On demand and accessible via web browser

Free Access for Packt account holders

If you have an account with Packt at www.PacktPub.com, you can use this to access PacktLib today and view nine entirely free books. Simply use your login credentials for immediate access.

Table of Contents

Preface

If you're relatively new to programming, or are just looking for a programming language that allows you to explore your visual and creative side, Scratch will be a lot of fun for you. Scratch was developed as a project of the Lifelong Kindergarten Group at the MIT Media Lab to make programming more accessible to young and/or new programmers.

As you work through this book, you'll gain a greater understanding of how to work with Scratch while simultaneously developing an understanding of fundamental programming principles that you'll want to know when you eventually begin to work with other programming languages.

You'll notice pretty quickly that this book is written focusing on Scratch 2.0, the newest version of Scratch. Don't worry though if you're still working in Scratch 1.4, the Scratch creators did a nice job keeping consistency between versions, so the differences won't be too challenging.

This book was written to be read in small bits at a leisurely pace or for an extended period of time in one sitting, it's up to you. Each chapter focuses on a specific aspect of Scratch and is broken down into easy to follow recipes. While most chapters make use of previous skills you've learned up to that point in the text, you don't necessarily need to read each chapter in order. Each recipe begins with the explicit steps you need to accomplish the goal of the recipe, follows with an explanation, then ends with some other ideas you may wish to explore on your own.

Lastly, the best way to learn Scratch (or any new programming language for that matter) is to not be afraid to play around as you go. Be sure to unleash your creative side; all you need is this book, a computer with Scratch, and your mind!

What this book covers

Chapter 1, *Getting Started with Scratch*, introduces the basics you'll need to know as you start working with Scratch. This chapter builds the foundation for the work done in all the other chapters and will help you get comfortable with Scratch.

Chapter 2, *Storytelling*, covers what you need to begin telling stories in Scratch, extending upon the animation techniques from.

Chapter 3, Adding Animation, tells us that Scratch is great for working with media; this is the chapter where you work with bringing some basic animation techniques into your programs.

Chapter 4, Basic Gaming, explains some of the first steps in creating a game in Scratch, as mostly everyone likes to create games.

Chapter 5, Spicing up Games, expands on the principles from the last chapter on games. This chapter spices things up while also bringing up some techniques you'll use for other programming.

Chapter 6, Bringing in Sound, covers adding and working with sounds in your programs.

Chapter 7, Integrating PicoBoards, explains how to get your sensor board working, as well as some fun programs to work with the board.

Chapter 8, Programming to Calculate, works with some of the techniques that make some tedious programming tasks easy.

Chapter 9, Project Remixing, covers taking projects in one form and transforming them. We'll examine this idea while also exploring other odds and ends in Scratch.

Appendix, Collaboration, covers how you can collaborate and share with other scratchers, as one great aspect in Scratch is to be able to share.

What you need for this book

We don't have to work with too much software for Scratch. We'll be working with Scratch 2.0 for the most part, which runs directly out of your browser. This requires any one of the following browsers:

- ▶ Chrome 7 or later
- ▶ Firefox 4 or later
- ▶ Internet Explorer 7 or later

Along with the browser, you should have Adobe Flash Player Version 10.2 installed (there is a good chance you already have all of this). If you don't have the ability to update your current software to meet these requirements, you can also download Scratch 1.4 from `http://scratch.mit.edu/scratch_1.4/`. We go into more detail on getting started with Scratch in the first chapter.

You can also find the requirements for using Scratch on your computer at `http://scratch.mit.edu/help/faq/`.

Who this book is for

This book is intended for a wide variety of audiences. You should be familiar with operating your computer pretty comfortably, and it would be helpful if you've seen Scratch before, though that is not required. If you've worked with Scratch quite a bit, it may be worthwhile to skip the first chapter, though there will be plenty to explore in the rest of the chapters.

More information

For extra book content, visit `http://www.bmilo.com/ScratchCookbook`.

Conventions

In this book, you will find a number of styles of text that distinguish between different kinds of information. Here are some examples of these styles, and an explanation of their meaning.

Code words in text, database table names, folder names, filenames, file extensions, pathnames, dummy URLs, user input, and Twitter handles are shown as follows. "You'll notice that we imported the first four that are available in the `Outdoors` folder, and deleted the default white background".

New terms and **important words** are shown in bold. Words that you see on the screen, in menus or dialog boxes for example, appear in the text like this: "Place a **forever** loop directly underneath, from the **Control** category".

For blocks where you as the programmer need to place a value, words, or something else, you'll notice we indicate that with parentheses. An example of this is the **move () steps** block from the **Motion** category.

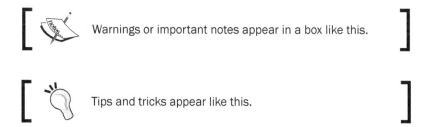

Reader feedback

Feedback from our readers is always welcome. Let us know what you think about this book—what you liked or may have disliked. Reader feedback is important for us to develop titles that you really get the most out of.

To send us general feedback, simply send an e-mail to `feedback@packtpub.com`, and mention the book title via the subject of your message.

If there is a topic that you have expertise in and you are interested in either writing or contributing to a book, see our author guide on `www.packtpub.com/authors`.

Customer support

Now that you are the proud owner of a Packt book, we have a number of things to help you to get the most from your purchase.

Errata

Although we have taken every care to ensure the accuracy of our content, mistakes do happen. If you find a mistake in one of our books—maybe a mistake in the text or the code—we would be grateful if you would report this to us. By doing so, you can save other readers from frustration and help us improve subsequent versions of this book. If you find any errata, please report them by visiting `http://www.packtpub.com/submit-errata`, selecting your book, clicking on the **errata submission form** link, and entering the details of your errata. Once your errata are verified, your submission will be accepted and the errata will be uploaded on our website, or added to any list of existing errata, under the Errata section of that title. Any existing errata can be viewed by selecting your title from `http://www.packtpub.com/support`.

Piracy

Piracy of copyright material on the Internet is an ongoing problem across all media. At Packt, we take the protection of our copyright and licenses very seriously. If you come across any illegal copies of our works, in any form, on the Internet, please provide us with the location address or website name immediately so that we can pursue a remedy.

Please contact us at `copyright@packtpub.com` with a link to the suspected pirated material.

We appreciate your help in protecting our authors, and our ability to bring you valuable content.

Questions

You can contact us at `questions@packtpub.com` if you are having a problem with any aspect of the book, and we will do our best to address it.

1
Getting Started with Scratch

In this chapter, we will cover the following recipes:

- ▸ Starting up Scratch
- ▸ Deleting the default sprite
- ▸ Adding a custom sprite
- ▸ Adding a pre-made sprite
- ▸ Changing the stage background
- ▸ The Hello World project

Introduction

This chapter explains all you need to know to get started when working with Scratch. We'll be focusing on using the latest version of Scratch, Scratch 2.0. Scratch gives young programmers the flexibility to develop programs of all types, many of which will be explored throughout this book. This chapter is meant to get you used to working with the Scratch interface before we dive into the more challenging topics involved. Note that if you have worked with Scratch some time before, you may wish to move on to *Chapter 2, Storytelling*. If you are new to Scratch, or have been away for quite some time, this chapter is just the right place to get started! For more information on getting started, it might be helpful to visit the Scratch resources at `http://scratch.mit.edu/help`.

Starting up Scratch

This first recipe to follow, which will help you download and install Scratch to your computer. Follow along and you'll be using Scratch in no time.

Getting ready

Our first recipe is all about getting Scratch up and running. Scratch can easily be used on any computer. Simply visit `http://scratch.mit.edu/help/faq/` to see the requirements for Scratch. If you've used Scratch 1.4 before, you'll recall that you had to install Scratch on your computer. The Scratch creators have made it even easier to use Scratch 2.0. Now you can run Scratch directly within your browser. All you need is a recent browser and Adobe Flash Player!

> Although Scratch can be installed on Mac, Windows, and Linux, in this book all of the instructions will be tailored to using a Windows-based system with Scratch 2.0. The commands should be the same, just keep this in mind if you are using a different system.

How to do it...

To use Scratch 2.0, simply click on the **Create** link on the Scratch home page. If you want to use Scratch 1.4, follow these steps. The installer will create a link on your desktop for you as well as a Start menu shortcut. Follow these steps to download and install Scratch:

1. Open your browser, and then visit `http://scratch.mit.edu/scratch_1.4/` to download the version of Scratch you need.

2. Click on the link to the appropriate version based on your operating system, as shown in the following screenshot:

Scratch 1.4 Download

Scratch Installer For Mac OS X
Compatible with Mac OSX 10.4 or later

MacScratch1.4.dmg

Scratch Installer for Windows
Compatible with Windows 2000, XP, Vista, 7, and 8

ScratchInstaller1.4.exe

See below for additional Windows options

Scratch Installer for Debian / Ubuntu
Compatible with Ubuntu 12.04 when backports are enabled

Install Scratch with Software Center
or download here

See the Scratch on Linux page for more information

We are pleased to provide Scratch free of charge. If you enjoy using Scratch, please consider making a donation to support future development of Scratch.

Want help getting started with Scratch?
Visit Getting Started with Scratch.

What's changed in the new version?
See the Scratch 1.4 Release Notes.

Having trouble with the Windows Installer?
Here's a files only version of Scratch 1.4 for Windows: WinScratch1.4.zip

Want to deploy Scratch on a Windows Network?
Here is the Scratch1.4.msi installer, updated 12/13/11. See the Network Installation page for more info.
Thanks to the makers of Advanced Installer for giving us a free license.

Have an older computer?
Try using an earlier version of Scratch.

Other questions?
See the Scratch FAQ.

3. Depending on your Internet connection speed, it may take a couple of minutes for Scratch to download.

4. Click on **Yes** on any prompts that come up confirming you want to open the file.

5. The Scratch installer will open. Click on **Next >** to begin the install process.

6. Next you'll be prompted to choose an install location. The default location will serve most people just fine.

7. Click on **Next >**.

8. Scratch will give you the option to choose a Start menu folder location. It will default to creating a new folder called **Scratch**. You may change this if you wish.

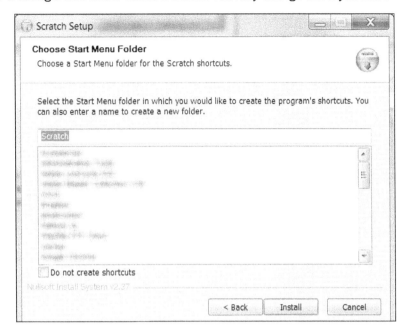

9. Click on **Install**.

10. Scratch will install, and then give you the following screenshot when finished:

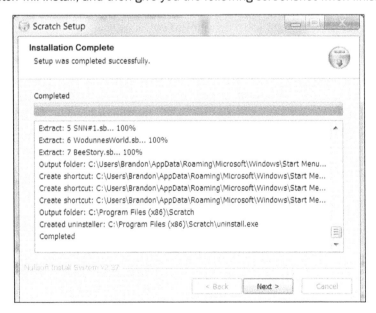

11. Click on **Next >**.

12. The final screen will give you the **Start Scratch** and **Make a shortcut to Scratch on the desktop** options.

13. Click on **Finish** and then you'll be ready to go!

How it works...

Once you're inside Scratch, play around with the interface. Scratch is broken up into three main areas that you'll be working in. These are called the **Block Palette**, **Script Area**, and **Stage**. These three areas are labeled in the following screenshot:

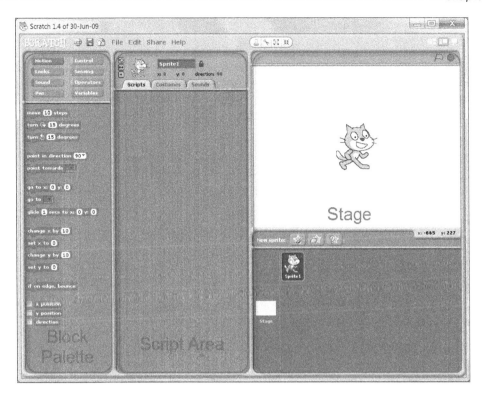

In Scratch 2.0, you'll see these areas in the following manner:

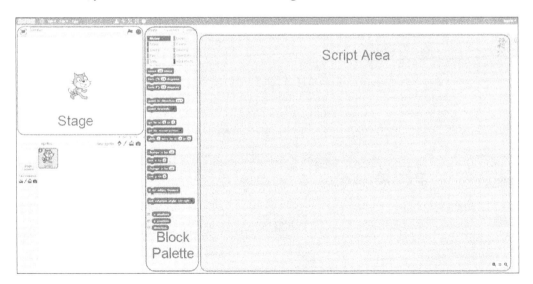

So, what are these three areas all about? How do I use them to build programs?

Each of these areas helps in a different way to build your program. The **Block Palette** is your library of commands, which you can add to your program. To build programs, all you need to do is drag and-drop these to your **Script Area**. Notice that there are eight categories of blocks. Each of these is color coded and does something different. We will explore more and more of these with each program we create!

The script area is vital to each individual program. A sprite is an object in Scratch we will program (usually characters). The default is the cat seen in the preceding screenshot. Each sprite as well as the background have their own **Script Area**, where you can drag blocks from the **Block Palette**. With more complicated programs, you need to drag more and more of these blocks to the **Script Area**.

A few examples of sprites you might use in your program are:

- ▸ Characters for a story or game
- ▸ Buttons to control things in your program
- ▸ Things you want to display on the stage, maybe digits for numbers that need to have background programming

The last area of the Scratch interface is probably your favorite: the **Stage**. Here is where everything you've programmed comes together, and then you can see it in action. Just below the Stage is the collection of all the sprites you've added to your program, this is how you select those individual script areas we mentioned before. Once we get past our first program, most of the magic will happen after you click on the green flag up in the right-hand corner of the stage. You can also stop everything by clicking on the little red button next to the green flag.

See also

Now that you have a basic understanding of the interface of Scratch, we can move on to customizing some of the fun things we'll be programming. Our next recipe, *Deleting the default sprite* features importing, adding, and changing sprites. See the rest of the recipes in this chapter as well for further basic information you'll need to program with Scratch.

Deleting the default sprite

As we mentioned before, sprites are the objects you program. They are the characters to your stories, players of your games, and everything in between. When you first open up Scratch, the default sprite is the cat (the one seen in the screenshot of the interface). You may want to use that sprite, or import a different one or more of them. We'll start by deleting the default sprite.

Getting ready

Later in this chapter, we are going to create our first program with Scratch: Hello World. All of our recipes in this chapter will lead up to this. Let's get this setup by customizing our environment. All you have to do to get this recipe ready is open up Scratch. This recipe is all about getting rid of the default sprite so that you can import others.

How to do it...

Follow through this series of steps to get rid of the default sprite that Scratch opens with:

1. Right-click on the sprite and choose the **delete** option.

2. You can also see a pair of scissors in the tools just above the stage, as shown in the following screenshot:

3. Click on the scissors icon.

4. Click on the sprite you wish to delete.

 You can use these tools in the script area as well with your programming blocks when you build your programs.

There's more...

You will notice with this set of tools above the stage, you have a few other fun options to work with. The first of these is the clone tool. Use this to copy sprites on your stage, so you don't have to reimport them (once we get to that, don't worry, it's coming!).

The third and fourth tools here are great in adjusting the size of your sprites. The first of these two increases the size (or grows) of your sprite. Similarly, the last tool decreases (or shrinks) your sprite. Each click increases or decreases the size by one level.

 As you progress through this book, don't go too far in reading without trying things on your computer! Take a minute now to test out the tools we've used so far and play around.

Adding a custom sprite

Now to the really fun part: adding in a new sprite! Directly below the stage area is a set of three buttons, as you can see in the following screenshot:

Each of these buttons helps us to import the sprites we want in our program. These are the buttons we'll work with for the next couple of recipes.

Getting ready

The second of these buttons gives you the best opportunity to bring out your creative side. This opens up the paint editor. From here, you can create your own sprite or import one of the sprites from the Scratch library, and then customize it. We won't get into a lot of depth to using it now, but if you're feeling to make your own sprite, take some time to play around.

In the preceding screenshot, you'll see the paint editor that gives you many of the functions that you have in the commonly known basic paint software that comes with your computer. In the beginning, it might be easier to use the **Import** button to bring in a sprite from the library. Then you can use the various paint cropping and drawing tools to make the sprite your own.

 One of the most useful aspects of the paint editor is the ability to use it to change the color of sprites. Not a fan of the yellow cat? Want to make a black cat for Halloween? Easy; just use a combination of the paint bucket and paint brush tools!

How to do it...

These are the steps we'll need to create a custom sprite (or customize one of the pre-made ones):

1. Click on the second of the buttons described previously.

2. The paint editor (shown in the previous screenshot) will open up.

3. Use the tools of the paint editor to create the sprite of your choice.

4. Click on **OK** once you've finished editing the sprite. Your sprite will now be in the stage.

Adding a pre-made sprite

This is one of the easiest ways to get programming quickly! The second of our buttons is called the **Choose new Sprite from File** button. This will open up a dialog box showing you all of the available sprites in the Scratch library.

You have many different sprites to choose from, including the categories of animals, fantasy, letters, people, things, and transportation.

 Remember, sprites are any objects you will be programming to do something in your overall program. In many cases, they will be characters in a story or in a game. In some cases, they may be buttons your user will interact with or some other general object. This is where the categories of letters or things come into play!

Getting ready

For the purposes of our first program, we'll choose one of the animals. You can choose whichever sprite you want, what matters is the programming we'll put into it later on.

How to do it...

Follow these steps and you'll have a new sprite to program within no time:

1. Click on the first button from the set of four shown in the following screenshot:

2. A dialogue box will pop up to select the sprite. Choose the folder for the type of sprite you want. Either double-click on the folder or click on **OK**.

3. Find the sprite you like and then click on **OK**.
4. The sprite will now be on the stage and ready to program with.

There's more...

The third button in the set we mentioned before allows us to upload a sprite from our computer. If you've created a picture of something on your own, you can use this tool to upload it. The last button allows us to take a picture using a webcam and then upload that as a sprite!

See also

- ▸ The *Starting up Scratch* recipe in this chapter
- ▸ The *Changing the stage background* recipe in this chapter

Changing the stage background

Once you've been programming in Scratch for a while, there is a good chance that you may need to change the background to something other than the default white color. Fortunately, Scratch makes this easy to do!

Getting ready

The area directly underneath the stage is where we select the sprite we are currently going to work on the programming for. You'll also notice that on the left side is an icon with a picture of the stage background (currently white if you haven't been straying from this chapter). This icon is labeled **stage**. Click on this.

If you've done anything in the script area with the sprite you had selected, you'll notice it is no longer visible in the script area. Whatever you do, don't worry. You have a different script area for each sprite as well as the stage.

You might be wondering what we are going to do with the script area for the stage. We won't use this for a while until we get into more advanced programs, but the stage script area is great for programming actions that will occur in the background of your program. Sometimes you may not have a block of programming that isn't specific to a particular sprite. This is where you will put that block.

How to do it...

So let's get rid of that boring background! Follow along with these steps!

1. In the stage script area, click on the second tab towards the top labelled **Backdrops**. You can import several backgrounds that you may later on want to access through programming blocks in your block palette. For now, let's just import a new one and delete the white background.

2. Similar to how we imported new sprites in three different ways; you have towards the top of the **Backdrops** tab three different options for backgrounds. The second of these brings up the paint editor. If you didn't take the time to get used to the paint editor when making your own sprite this may be a great time to create a background. You can add any colors you want, shapes, or imported images.

 Don't import a sprite when creating your own background. If you do, be careful. You may later on try to drag the sprite, thinking it's an actual sprite in your program. This will leave you confused (and possibly frustrated) when you can't get something to work.

3. If you didn't go down the route of creating your own background, then you can choose the very common import button. Just like the sprite library, you have categories. The categories for your pre-made backgrounds are indoors, nature, outdoors, and sports. You also have an x-y grid you can use if you are getting into some fun with math.

 Not happy with the backgrounds available? Don't want to make your own? The dialog box that comes up just points to the folder on your computer where Scratch has put these pre-made designs when it was installed. You can access your pictures on other parts of your computer just as you would in any other software package on your computer.

4. The third option is to upload an image directly from your computer.

5. The fourth option you have is to access your computer's webcam and take a picture. Clicking on the camera option will pop up the webcam of your computer. Click on the picture of the camera and you should see your webcam's image pop into the background!

6. Once you've selected your new background, you'll see it added to the list of backgrounds available to program with. It should look something similar to the following screenshot:

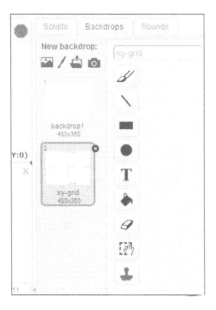

There's more...

To delete the white background we won't need, click the small circle containing an **x**.

Notice that you can edit or copy backgrounds. This gives you the functionality to customize backgrounds and make them your own. Also, notice that you can change the given name of a background (the default seen in the preceding screenshot is background1). As you build more complicated programs, it may be beneficial to give these names you'll recognize throughout the program. You might find it useful to do the same thing with your sprites; we'll bring this up again later though.

Now that you have a new sprite and a new background, we are ready to create our first program. We may not have a fancy game yet, but it's enough to get us acquainted with Scratch and ready for our next steps.

See also

▸ The _Hello World project_ recipe in this chapter.

The Hello World project

If you've done much programming before, you may have already seen a program similar to this. If this is your first time programming and you go on to learn more, it is likely you'll get used to doing many of these types of programs. It is customary in many programming packages for your first experience to be a Hello World program.

Getting ready

This is a rather simple program that we'll work with for the rest of the chapter to get us settled in Scratch. Our first task is to get our sprite to tell the world "hello". From there, we'll do a few other fun things.

How to do it...

Follow these steps:

1. Use the background and sprite you imported from earlier in the chapter or import new ones; it's up to you!

2. Activate the script area you need by clicking on the sprite you have in the program in the area below the stage (not the stage itself). If you were working with backgrounds above, you may need to go to the script area, and then change the tab from **Costumes** to **Scripts**.

3. Next, we need to work with the block palette to build our program. First we'll give the sprite the functionality to output hello world to the screen. Remember the **Block palette** we talked about in the beginning of the chapter? Now it's the time to put it in use. Click on the second category of blocks labeled **Looks**. These purple blocks handle anything to do with the appearance of your sprite.

4. Now from the **Looks** category, click and hold the block to the script area.

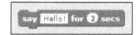

5. Click on the area that has the word **Hello!**, and then change this to say **Hello World!**. If you want, you can also change the **2** to any other number you'd like. This number **2** represents the amount of time our message will be displayed.

6. Try double-clicking on your newly added block. Watch the stage. Your sprite will display the message, and you have created your very first program. Don't worry; they get much more fun as we go along!

   Let's continue by adding a control block to our script.

7. Choose the **Events** category. Drag over the first block in this category and drop it right on top of the **Looks** block we already placed on the stage.

   They look together as puzzle pieces, and you'll see a white line as you hover over the spot (which Scratch is anticipating you will drop the block onto). This can be tremendously useful once you get into having several blocks within others.

 The preceding screenshot is known as a top-hat block. It gets its name from being like a top-hat and going on top of a script. These top-hat blocks are ones that start of a sequence of programming and can't be built on from above. Almost all of the blocks from the **Events** category are top-hat blocks.

8. Now that we have the "When green flagged clicked" block in our program, we no longer have to double-click on the script to run the script. If you click on the green flag on the stage, everything underneath the When green flag clicked block will run for us. We'll start most of our programs this way, so that we'll get accustomed to just dragging it in quite often.

How it works...

So, what is happening behind the scenes right now in our program? Basically, when we click on the green flag on our stage, this sends a signal throughout the program that is received by the When green flag clicked block (known as a listener). Once this listener is activated, the program sequentially works through the list of commands connected to the When green flag clicked block until they are all completed. Once finished, the program is done. As you'll see in some of our programs later, you can have as many of these listener blocks in your program as you want. You can then run multiple parts of your program simultaneously.

There's more...

Now that we have this basic program, why not make it a little more interesting? Scratch gives us so many ways we can do just that! Let's take the chance now to add a bit more to our Hello World program.

Saving your work in any type of programming you do is important! Stop now and change the name shown above the stage to something you'll remember. By default, Scratch saves to your own project folder on the Scratch website. Give the file a name. If you view the project page, you can add notes and instructions to your project.

Adding some motion

The next thing we'll do is make our sprite move across the stage. Under the **Motion** category of blocks in the block palette, grab the first block and drag it underneath the current set of blocks you have. It looks similar to the following screenshot:

You now have three blocks in your script for this program. The following are the steps to be performed to move our sprite across the stage:

Click on the green flag on the stage. You should see your sprite greeting you with the **Hello World!** phrase from before, and then move the sprite a small amount to the right.

Movement to the right is denoted by positive numbers, and movement to the left is denoted by negative numbers (unless of course you change the sprite's direction using other motion blocks). An easy way to think of it is the comparison to an x-y coordinate plane; it works the same way.

We can continue to press the green flag and our sprite will move. Experiment a bit with the value in the motion block you just added. Change it to a larger number, then maybe even a negative number.

What if we want our sprite to keep moving though once we press the green flag? This part is easy! We're going to introduce a new block that you're going to learn to use quite a bit when you program. Under the control set of blocks, you'll see the one that is labeled **forever**. It looks as though it wraps around something, and it does! We're going to call this a forever loop.

A forever loop is also called sometimes an infinite loop in programming. Once you get into higher-level languages, you might find an infinite loop to be trouble. Can you guess why? It's because if you make a complicated enough program, you may not know when the infinite loop is continuing forever, so it has the potential to wreak havoc on your program. It's hard for that to be an issue in Scratch, though, so we won't worry too much about that for now.

Drag this **forever** loop into your program. As you drag, essentially try and place it between the looks block you added and the motion block. The **forever** loop will expand as you hover, so it looks like it will wrap around the motion block.

Your code should now look similar to the following screenshot:

Try pressing the green flag and see what happens. Your sprite should move to the end of the stage and then stop. Our goal is to get our sprite to bounce off the screen and then go back and forth.

In the **Motion** blocks, we'll see another block we can use to make this happen. It's called the **if on edge, bounce** block, which is towards the bottom of the list. Drag this block directly underneath the **move 10 steps** block we've added already, and still in the **forever** loop. You should immediately see your sprite begin to bounce back and forth on the stage. If not, try clicking on the green flag button again.

Special sprite settings

You've probably noticed by now that your sprite isn't staying upright as it bounces across the screen. Scratch has some easy settings to fix this. On your sprite, if you want to access settings (shown beneath the stage), click on the small blue icon in the corner. You'll see the following screenshot:

Here we have several bits of information that can be helpful in building our programs. Notice the three buttons to the left of the picture of your sprite. The following are the ways in which these buttons affect the orientation of your sprite:

▸ If you click on the first button, your sprite will be able to rotate when it bounces off of objects such as the edge of the screen. This is the default for every sprite in Scratch.

▸ If you click on the second button, this fixes the orientation of your sprite such that it will only face back and forth. Click on this one for our Hello World program; your sprite should straighten out and then move across the screen as you would expect an animal or person to do.

▸ The last one fixes the orientation of your sprite completely. It won't change the direction the sprite will be looking, and your sprite won't go upside down at all. This may be useful in future games we make where we want fixed objects moving.

Now we'll examine a few of the other things that are in the sprite settings area. The first of these is the label for the sprite, ours is currently labeled **Sprite1**. You can change this name to anything you want that might make it easier to identify throughout your program. This is particularly helpful when you make a more complicated program that has many more sprites to keep track of.

Also, take a look at the three numbers below the sprite label. Two of these, the x and y values, tell you the location of your sprite on the stage. Remember how we said the stage is essentially a coordinate plane? Think of the center as the origin where **x: 0** and **y: 0**. Negative values move to the left (or down for y) and positive values move to the right (or up for y). You also see a **direction** label. This tells you the direction your sprite is currently facing in degrees.

Before proceeding with the next part, try changing the number of steps your sprite moves within the loop. Change the number first from 10 to something higher, and then try a lower number between 1 and 10. You'll see this adjusts the speed of your sprite when it's in the loop. This is because the sprite moves the number of steps you set and then continues to repeat. By increasing the number you are increasing the number of steps that occur only one time through the loop, but not increasing the time it takes. As a result, your sprite speeds up. This works the same way in decreasing your speed with a lower number of steps.

Pointing towards the mouse

Now let's say instead of our sprite just bouncing back and forth on the screen, we want to have it follow our mouse. This can be a nice addition to our program, and may come in handy in future programs we make.

The following are the steps we have to do in order to accomplish this:

1. Drag in a new block from our **Block palette**. Notice the **Motion** block that says **point towards** has an empty space. Click on the down arrow in this empty space, and then select **mouse pointer**.

2. Now drag this block into the program directly underneath the **if on edge, bounce** block.

 If you have other sprites in your program, you can change the **point towards** block to point at other sprites in the program. This might come in handy in later programs where we have objects "chasing" other objects.

3. Now run your program by clicking on the green flag. Move your mouse around the stage; and your sprite will follow the pointer.

 A convention we'll use in this book for blocks such as the block we just used is to indicate with parentheses customizable areas such as blank spaces or drop-down selections. For example, for the last block, we'd refer to it as the **point towards** block.

Duplicating code

It's not going to take too long for us to add more and more sprites to our programs. Let's learn how to do this now while we're still getting started. There are two ways to accomplish this:

Our first task is to copy code to a new sprite. The following are the steps to perform this task:

1. Begin by importing a new sprite into your program. Recall from above how to do this.

2. Once you have a new sprite, keep the script area from the original sprite selected and then click and hold the top-hat block containing all of our code so far.

3. Drag this over the area underneath the stage showing all of the sprites.

4. Drop the code on top of the new sprite.

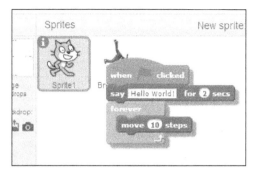

It won't look similar to what had happened before, but you'll be able to click on the new sprite now and see that the exact code you just dragged in is duplicated there. This can be a great method to duplicate code you need for many sprites.

Run your program and test what we've done. You should see both sprites greeting the world, and then follow your mouse pointer around the stage.

Now we can also consider a situation where we might want to duplicate the code within a sprite. This part isn't really necessary for our Hello World program, but it is nice to know how to perform this using the following steps:

1. Remember those four buttons we talked about above the stage? The first one is a clone tool. Click on this tool, and then click on the part of the code you wish to duplicate. This can either be the top-hat block containing all of the code, or just some of the blocks below it.

2. As you move your mouse, you'll see that you are dragging a copy of the code you just clicked. Click anywhere in the script area to drop the code. If you were duplicating just a piece of code (note that because we used a forever loop, we can't do this part now), you can add it to the bottom of the code you are copying. If you have repetitive actions that need to occur in sequence, this can be an easy way of copying code quickly.

3. Try adjusting your program a bit to get used to Scratch.

4. Select the script area of your second sprite and change the number of steps per loop that run. If your first sprite is still set to **10**, change the other sprite to something (for example, **2** or **3**). Experimenting with various blocks and programs we develop here in this book will be a great way to become a Scratch expert pretty quickly.

We've done a lot of introductory tasks to get our Hello World program working in this chapter. You should now have a good understanding of the basics that you need to complete everything in this book. Each chapter will lead you into a different aspect of programming with Scratch, many of which will get you into more and more advanced programs as you go. As it was mentioned before, be sure to follow along near your computer and work with Scratch as you go. Practicing as you go helps you build your skills much better than just reading along.

Most importantly, have fun!

See also

This chapter is focused on the basics you'll need to get going in Scratch. In our next chapter we're going to focus on getting you ready to use Scratch to tell stories. If you're not looking to tell stories, it still may be useful to look over some of the recipes in *Chapter 2, Storytelling* to prepare you for using some of those techniques in other things we'll do later on in the book.

2
Storytelling

In this chapter, we will cover:

- ▸ Adding words to a sprite
- ▸ Adjusting the timing
- ▸ Sprites interacting with other sprites
- ▸ Basic broadcasting and receiving
- ▸ Resetting parts of a program
- ▸ Other fun graphic effects

Introduction

In the previous chapter, you learned about a lot of different basic things that we can do with Scratch. You learned specifically about the Scratch interface and created your first project, incorporating control and movement blocks. This chapter will focus on how you can use Scratch to tell a story.

We'll primarily be interested in learning more about the **Looks** blocks, **Control** blocks, and **Events** blocks. Take a look at each recipe to get a good understanding of these types of blocks. While these recipes focus on storytelling, we'll use a lot of these concepts in later chapters as well, for other types of projects we make.

Adding words to a sprite

One of the first things we need to know to tell a story using Scratch is to display words on the screen to convey the story. For this recipe, we'll need to use some of the concepts we learned in the previous chapter.

Getting ready

Start off by importing a new sprite (unless you like the default) as well as a background you like. Also, start thinking about a story you want to tell—or you can just follow what we do here!

There are two blocks that we are going to use to accomplish all of this, one of which we used already in the previous chapter. This family of blocks are the **say** and **think** blocks:

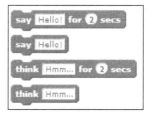

Recall that the first one in this list is the block we used in the previous chapter.

So what's the difference between all of these blocks?

Two of these blocks help with timing. These are the first and third in the picture that include a time condition. These are the ones we will focus on because we generally want to control how long the words are displayed on the screen.

The story we are going to make here is going to be told by Monkey Mike. We labeled our sprite this to make understanding the logic of the programming a bit easier.

Now we're ready to get building a story!

How to do it...

Follow these steps to get going:

1. Drag over the block with the green flag that we used to start our programs in the previous chapter from the **Events** category. We'll start our story by clicking on the green flag on the stage.

Still using the older version of Scratch (Scratch 1.4)? All of the blocks in the **Events** category can be found in the **Control** category. This new category was added with the new version of Scratch.

2. Next, we're going to return to the **Looks** block category and drag over the **think** block, the first one including the timing.

3. Enter **Hmm...I guess I'll start telling a story.** into the text block.

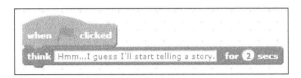

4. Click on the green flag and test the program. You should see a thought bubble pop up as if your sprite is thinking. It should be similar to the following screenshot, depending of course on the background and sprite you chose:

 You may wish to adjust the number of seconds for which the thought bubble appears. You do this by changing the number associated with the **think** block in the code. Enter the number of seconds it shows for how long you expect your viewer to need to read the text. The same rule applies for other texts being displayed.

5. Now, we can drag in our next block—the **say** block—again including the timing element.

> You might be wondering what is the difference between the **say** and **think** blocks. Both accomplish similar goals. You can think of them as cartoons. The **think** block imitates the thoughts of the character while the **say** block suggests that the character is saying something. Note that neither makes the character make a noise.

6. Enter the text in this block as **Hi, my name is Monkey Mike**. We can continue creating a basic story by adding more and more of these blocks to our code.

> If you want to end your story with the text remaining on the screen, just use the **say** or **think** block without the timing element. This will keep the text on the screen until the viewer either starts the program over or does something else to trigger it (we'll learn more about this option later).

How it works...

So far, this program is relatively simple. Our code so far is:

We can see this sequence of code starting off with the green flag being clicked. Following that, our sprite thinks about starting the story, and then he begins. Naturally, your program may vary depending on how much you've digressed from the story we are using here.

See also

▶ For more information about timing your story, particularly with multiple sprites in the story, see the next recipe, *Adjusting the timing*

Adjusting the timing

There is a good chance that the story you have in mind includes more than one sprite. This means that you are also going to need to think about timing in your story since you don't want to have both sprites talking at the same time.

> Timing can become more and more complex depending on the program, especially as you add more and more sprites and length to your story. A good way to handle this situation is to think ahead of time as to when you want your sprite to speak, and when you want them to simply observe. Having this planned out will help you program much more quickly.

Getting ready

Continuing with our existing story, add another sprite. For example, we added a frog to our program in the bottom center. Copy over the same code (that we used for the first sprite) to make the second sprite think and talk. Note that if you duplicated the sprite, this is done for you. You'll notice both of them talking at the same time, which is what we are going to learn to fix (see the following screenshot showing roughly what you should see). Our example is relatively simple, but you can apply this concept to even the most complicated Scratch programs.

> Remember, you don't need to recreate the code for the new sprite. With the original sprite selected, click and drag all of the code (beginning with the top hat block) on top of the picture icon of the sprite located below the stage. Your code should then appear in the script area of both sprites.

This is what you should see when you run your program:

How to do it...

Our next step is to get the timing right, and then we'll worry about making our characters say something different from each other. Follow these steps:

1. For our story, we want Monkey Mike to start things off and have Frog follow. We know that Monkey Mike thinks for two seconds, so there needs to be a delay of at least two seconds on what Frog thinks. Notice that in the **Control** blocks we have a block called **wait 1 secs** with the **1** being an input box for you to change the number. While working in the script area for Frog, drag over the wait block and place it directly underneath the block with the green flag, as shown in the following screenshot:

2. Next, change the value in the block you just dragged over to **2** instead of **1**.

3. Now, we'll want to add another wait block in between the **think** and **say** blocks we have for Frog. Make this block **2** seconds long as well.

4. If you run your program now, you'll still notice a bit of a problem. We still need to make Monkey Mike wait while Frog is talking. Return to the script area for Monkey Mike. Place a wait block in between the **think** and **say** blocks, just as we did for Frog. Change this value to **2** as well.

5. Now, change the text of Frog's thought bubble to **I wonder if Monkey Mike notices me down here**. Then, change the **say** block to **Hi, you can just call me Frog**.

6. Run your program and see what happens. It should flow much better now that we've adjusted the timing.

How it works...

So now you're probably wondering what is happening behind the scenes. Let's look at the two pieces of code.

Our code for Monkey Mike is shown here:

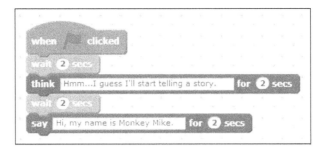

And here is the code for Frog:

The biggest thing to notice in thinking about how the script runs in our program is that since both scripts begin with the block with the green flag, both scripts start simultaneously.

 In essence, you can have an unlimited number of scripts running simultaneously in Scratch. We'll learn soon how to get different scripts started with other **Events** blocks. This will give us much more control over our programs.

While we may have made it appear—when watching the story—that the sprites are waiting for each other, really what is happening is that each script is playing independently of the other. We just adjusted the timing effectively to give the story the timing we want.

There's more...

Maybe you don't want to have to click on the green flag to start the story. An alternative is to use the **when key pressed** top hat block instead, also from the **Events** category:

If you replace the green flag block with this new block, your story will start by pressing a specific key on the keyboard. By default, the block is triggered by the Space bar. You can change this by clicking on the black down arrow located next to the word **space**.

You'll see that this is the block we will use quite frequently (to get different aspects of our program to start) when we get into creating games and other programs.

For now, we'll stick with using the standard green-flag block for most script starting, but think of this as a good alternative in your own programming.

See also

▸ For more details on timing, see the *Adding words to a sprite* recipe

▸ To see how to get your sprites to interact, take a look at our next recipe, *Sprites interacting with other sprites*

▸ Later in this chapter in the *Basic broadcasting and receiving* recipe, we'll explore a fun way to get background communication in your program

Sprites interacting with other sprites

When making your story, there is a good chance you will want to get movement on the stage so your story is a bit more exciting. This recipe focuses on how to have sprites react when they are touching or moving around other sprites.

Getting ready

For this recipe, we're going to continue working with the story we built in our previous recipes of this chapter. Our goal for this recipe is to get Frog to move across the screen and react to Monkey Mike when they touch.

How to do it...

We're going to bring back some scripting from our first chapter to get the job done. Let's get started:

1. To begin the movement of Frog, the user will have to click on the sprite. We'll need to provide directions to the user in order to accomplish this. At the end of Frog's dialogue (from before), add another **say** block and give it the text `Click me to get me moving`.

2. Now we'll introduce a new top hat block. This is the **when this sprite clicked** block, located under the **Events** blocks category. It changes based on the sprite you are working on, so for ours it should indicate you are working with Frog.

3. We'll drag this block over and begin a new script in the script area. We are going to get horizontal movement going on Frog, the same way we did in *Chapter 1, Getting Started with Scratch*.

4. Drag over a **forever** loop from the **Control** blocks underneath our new top hat block.

5. Place a **move 10 steps** block (from **Motion**) and the **if on edge, bounce** block (also from **Motion**) into the **forever** loop.

   Change the number of steps to something low, such as the number **2**, to make sure the sprite moves slowly.

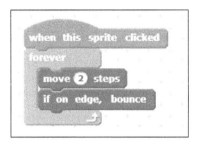

6. Recall also from the previous chapter that we need to change the sprite settings for Frog so that the sprite remains oriented the way it is and does not flip upside down as he bounces on the edge of the screen. Select the second orientation option in the 3-button option area of the sprite settings, as shown in the following screenshot.

   First we have to click on the settings option:

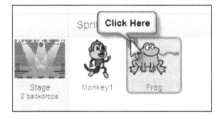

And then:

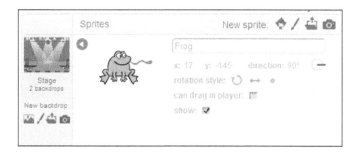

7. Now, if we run our program and click on Frog on the stage, we'll see Frog move slowly back and forth across the stage. Our next step will be to have the sprites interact when they touch.

8. We want Monkey Mike to react when Frog comes in front of him. In order to do this, we'll need to head over to the **Sensing** category of blocks. We'll also need a new **Control** block. Change the sprite we are working with to be Monkey Mike.

9. Underneath the dialog of Monkey Mike, drag over the **forever** block. This block is going to be triggered by a new sensing block.

10. Into the loop you created in step 9, drag an **if () then** block.

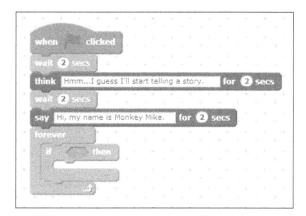

 If you are working in Scratch 1.4, steps 9 and 10 can be combined by using the **forever if** block. This block was eliminated in the new version of Scratch.

11. Drag over the **touching** block inside the look you just created, as shown in the following screenshot:

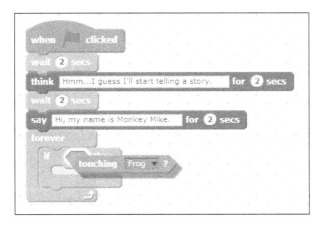

12. Change the **touching** block by clicking on the black drop-down arrow and selecting **Frog**.

 You can use the **touching** block to sense when your sprite is touching any other sprite, or the mouse-pointer, or an edge. This will be very useful when we get into more advanced topics in later chapters.

13. Now we need to make Monkey Mike say something when he is "touched" by Frog. Drag in the **say** block (with time element) and drop it within the **forever** block.

14. Change the text to say **Hey Frog, don't block my view**.

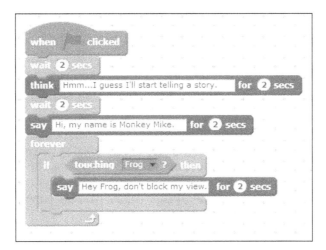

15. Now run your program to give it a test! Frog will pass in front of Monkey Mike and Monkey Mike will state his observation that Frog is in his way. This will continue as long as you let it go.

How it works...

We have several important ideas of programming going on in this recipe. We've already discussed the movement in *Chapter 1, Getting Started with Scratch*, so we will assume you are good to go with that.

As in our previous recipes, we have several scripts—all running at once. We learned about a new block, the **when this sprite clicked** block. This block is similar to our other top hat blocks in that it starts off a script. You can always use this block to start something when you want that particular sprite to be clicked. This only applies to the specific sprite you are programming though, so if you want to click on Frog and have something happen to Monkey Mike, you'll have to use a workaround (we'll talk about this in the next recipe).

Now let's take a look at the script for Monkey Mike. You should have something like the following screenshot:

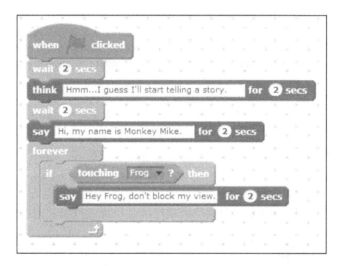

Once Monkey Mike finishes his dialog at the start of the story, he waits for Frog to pass by his field of vision. This block is essentially a combination of two other **Control** blocks available to us, so saves us time in terms of coding. We also have, available for use, the **forever** loop, which we've used before. Secondly, there is the `if` block. Any block with an if embedded creates an if statement, which is triggered when the statement is true. Our combined block that we used makes Monkey Mike constantly look for that statement to be true, and then repeats the code inside until the story is manually stopped.

If you are extending the story and still want Monkey Mike to say something about Frog passing by, you'll have to create a separate script to handle the **forever if** loop. This method of creating the code works well when you want nothing else added. However, now you can't add more talking after the loop. Also note that if your Frog isn't large enough, or close enough to the monkey, part of this code will never need to run.

There's more...

Perhaps we don't want Monkey Mike to comment on Frog passing by for the entire story—after all, there is a good chance this will affect how your story flows. We also have the option of using another block combination as an alternative.

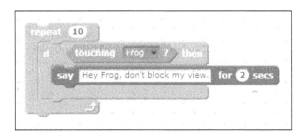

Here, we see that we can integrate the `repeat` loop and the `if` loop to create a loop that looks for the trigger a certain number of times—in our case 10. You can change this number if you want to something lower or something higher.

The logic of this section of code isn't too complicated. We see that the repeat loop continues what is inside it, 10 times. In other words, our code will check the condition we set (that is, whether or not we are touching Frog) 10 times, and then will stop checking and move on to whatever else we tack onto this script.

See also

▶ To see more ways for sprites to interact, check out the next recipe, *Basic broadcasting and receiving*. This recipe will teach you a lot about basic techniques of background communication that we'll need to use in future projects.

Basic broadcasting and receiving

Broadcasting and receiving is conceptually one of the most challenging ideas we've gotten to so far. That's because the idea is slightly more abstract than some of the other things we've discussed. Let's first talk a little about the principle it is built on, and then go into how it works in Scratch.

Getting ready

We have two separate ideas to think about. The first is the idea of broadcasting. Think of it as a radio station that sends out a signal that only radios can hear. If you are walking around outside, you're not going to hear anything. If you turn on a radio though, you can hear everything being broadcast. Receiving is kind of like the radio. It listens for a specific signal being broadcast, and then will trigger the code placed under it.

In Scratch, we have two blocks that act in this way. The **broadcast** block and the **when I receive** block, both of which are **Events** blocks. We'll talk more about these in the *How it works...* section coming up.

For this recipe, we will continue using the same Scratch program we have been working with for this chapter. Start off by matching your code with the following two sprites.

Our code for Monkey Mike:

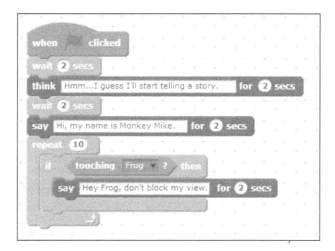

And the code for Frog should be:

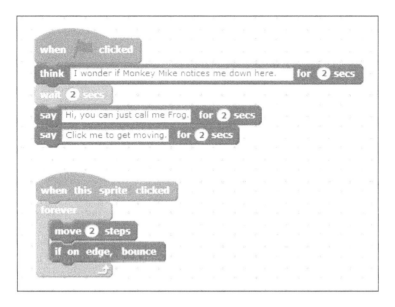

Now that you have caught up with us, we're going to have Monkey Mike introduce Frog as the storyteller, and then broadcast to Frog to begin the story.

How to do it...

Follow these steps to program Monkey Mike and Frog:

1. Have your Monkey Mike script ready to program.

2. At the end of the current script that we have, drag over a **say** block (with the time element) from the **Looks** category.

3. Type the text **Frog will now tell the story.** into the block from step 2.

4. Return to the **Events** blocks. We will now drag over the **broadcast** and **wait** blocks to the end of the sequence of code.

5. Click on the drop-down arrow next to the block you just dragged over and select **new message....**

6. A dialog box will appear. Enter the message name (that you want to broadcast) as **Start Story**.

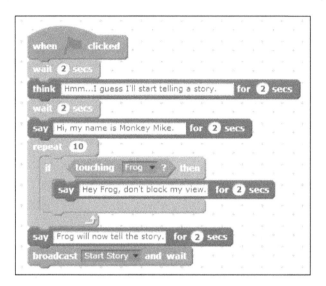

 The message name is only for making your code clear to others who look at it or for yourself later. Make it something simple, and something you'll recognize.

7. Since we used the version of broadcast that waits for the end of the sequence it starts, we'll need to plan for Monkey Mike to do something when the story is finished. Drag over another **say** block and add the text **That was a good story, Frog.** to the block.

8. Now that we have finished our broadcast message coming from Monkey Mike, we need to turn our attention to Frog. Be sure you have the script area of Frog selected and look in the **Events** blocks.

9. Drag over the top hat block that says **when I receive**. Since we already created a broadcast message, you'll see **Start Story** already filled in for us.

10. Now add enough **say** blocks to tell the story you want to tell. Your overall stack for the **when I receive** block should look like the following, customized for your own story of course:

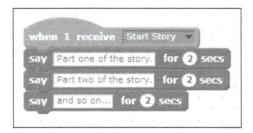

11. Now, test out your program. You should see what we had before, in addition to Frog telling our "story," with Monkey Mike concluding at the end.

 Looking for a better way to view your story? Notice that there is a button just above the stage. This adjusts the interface and brings the stage to full screen. When you want to test your program and don't need to see any code, choose this option to maximize the stage size.

How it works...

First we'll talk about the **broadcast** and **receive** blocks.

The broadcast block

The **broadcast** block has two forms, both of them shown here:

The first of the **broadcast** blocks simply broadcasts a message. This message is just like when a radio station sends out a signal that only radios can interpret. Thus, the message can only be interpreted in Scratch in a certain way.

The second block sends out a message—just as the first one does—but then waits for everything associated with that message to be completed before continuing the sequence of the program. This will make more sense once you see how this block is used, particularly with the **receive** block.

The receive block

Our **receive** block acts somewhat like the radio. It is a top hat block, so triggers a sequence of code just like the green-flag block and other top hat blocks we've worked with so far. This block is a **listener**. A listener does just what its name suggests; it listens in the background and waits for some event to occur. In this case, that event is some sort of broadcast sent somewhere else in the program. You'll see that whenever you have one of these blocks, either **broadcast** or **receive**, you need to have at least one of the other blocks, else nothing will happen.

More about the code

There are two main pieces to this code to understand what is going on in the background. The first of this is what happens with Monkey Mike. Monkey Mike gets the process started by broadcasting the message **Start Story**. Built into Frog's code we have a listener, the **when I receive (Start Story)** block. When the listener is triggered by the broadcast from Monkey Mike, the sequence of code connected to the listener (our story) begins to run. The **broadcast** block we had back in Monkey Mike's code waits until this code is finished. Once it's finished, Monkey Mike continues with what is left to that sequence of code. In our case, all that remains then is to end the story with his final statement.

Keep in mind that we can have multiple **receive** blocks working on one message. For instance, the broadcast can be sent and two **receive** blocks (in different sprites or the same sprites, doesn't matter) pick up the message and begin running a sequence of code.

There's more...

We can use our `broadcast` and `receive` commands to do any number of things. Let's take a moment to examine two other possibilities here.

Triggering an event with a click

In the previous recipe, we mentioned that you can only use the **when this sprite clicked** top hat block on the particular sprite being programmed, and not on others. We can use broadcasting and receiving to get around this.

For example, let's assume for a moment that you want to click anywhere on the stage to get Frog to begin moving. Set the visible script area to the stage and drag over the top hat block **when this sprite clicked**. Underneath this, drag over a new **broadcast** block (this time, use the one without the `wait` command). Click on the drop-down arrow and select **New**. Give this message the name **Move**.

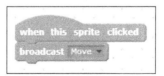

Return to the program for Frog and drag over the **when I receive** block to the script area. Make sure the message you just created, **Move**, is selected. Now, right-click on the **forever** loop we created previously for movement and select **duplicate** (as shown in the following screenshot).

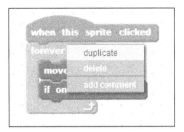

A copy of this sequence of code will appear. Drop it below our new top hat block to have the sequence as shown here:

If you run your program now, you will notice that if you click on the stage as well as Frog, Frog will move faster. This is a result of both scripts running at once, and so the speed is doubled. If you're worried about the speed varying like this, the best suggestion is to not have both sets of code in your program. Since these pieces of code are independent, we cannot (easily) stop one from running.

You can now use this technique to work around clicking on one object and having the code specifically on that object.

Changing the background

What if at some point in your story you want to change the background? Perhaps we can set this to happen when Monkey Mike announces that Frog will tell the story. Recall that we mentioned you can have multiple pieces of receive commands from a single broadcast.

Return to the script area for our stage. Drag over another **when I receive** block and change the message the block is receiving to **Start Story**. Next, take a look at your block palette and change the category to **Looks**. You'll notice that the category appears different for the stage than it does when you are working with a sprite.

Drag over the **switch backdrop to ()** block, the first one in the list, and connect it to the **when I receive** block that you just dragged over. To make this block effective, you need to select the **Backdrops** tab and be sure that there is a second background in your program. In our case, we'll select **Import** and navigate to the bench in a park, as shown in the following screenshot. Then select **OK**.

The background will automatically change to the new image you just imported, so you'll want to click on the first background to switch back.

Now return to the script area for the stage and adjust the **switch backdrop to** block to indicate a switch to the new image that we just imported. Now when we run our project, when the story begins, the setting will change to the park.

We should also note that we should drag one more piece of code into the stage area. It is worth noting that we can place this code in any sprite, but it is a common practice to put it in the stage since that is the most relevant area of the program for it.

Drag in a **when green flag clicked** block as well as the **switch to background** block. In the block that switches the background, ensure that the original background is selected. By adding this piece of code, you'll be resetting the background to your original image each time you start the story.

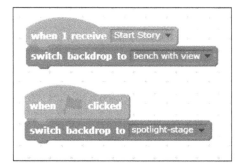

 Later on when we work with what are called variables, we will call this procedure of resetting things declaring variables. This process ensures that the program starts the same way every time. For instance, in games where we are keeping a tab on the score, we'll want to reset that score to 0 each time someone plays the game.

See also

- See the next recipe, *Resetting parts of a program*, for a quick description of what other things need to be reset in this story

- We'll explore more graphic effects in the final recipe of this chapter, *Other fun graphic effects*

Resetting parts of a program

This recipe introduces, more formally, what we did at the end of the previous recipe when we began the process of resetting aspects of our story. Sometimes when we have a program running various settings, placement of objects, variables, and so on, are going to get changed. When we run the program next time, we'll want all of those things to start from where we originally had them.

Getting ready

The example that we'll go through here is resetting the placement of Frog on the stage. This way, each time you click on the green flag, Frog will return to the same starting position.

How to do it...

To get this started, follow these steps:

1. Drag Frog (on the stage) to the place where you would like him to start each time the program runs. Examine the script -area settings and note the **x:** and **y:** positions that are given. From the following screenshot, we can see that Frog has an x -value of **18** and a y -value of **-145**:

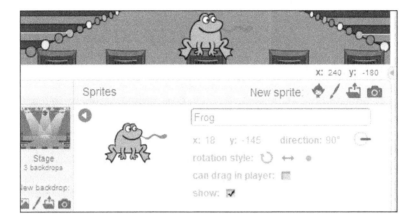

2. We'll need to know these numbers in just a moment. To reset the position of Frog each time, drag over a new green -flag block.

3. Connect to this the **go to x: y:** block in the **Motion** category. Most likely, the numbers filled in match the location where your Frog is now. If not, just change the numbers to match what our screenshot has here.

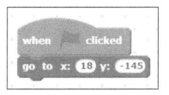

 This new block is a different way to get movement. Remember when we said the stage can be thought of as a coordinate plane from math class? This block tells the sprite to go to a particular location on the stage. You won't see this one take any "steps" as we've seen with other movements. Actually, since your computer is pretty fast, you might not notice anything but the location of the sprite change!

How it works...

Programmatically, this recipe doesn't change a whole lot in the program. The main purpose is to ensure that everything starts uniformly no matter who is watching and controlling our program. This is a technique we'll use quite often throughout the rest of this book. It is also a common practice in other programming languages to declare variables (or as in this case, more like just resetting things).

There's more...

What if you wanted the movement to be noticeable? Not a problem! You can see that just a couple of blocks below the **go to** block is a **glide** block. Inputs to this **glide** block include the number of seconds in addition to the x-y coordinates, similar to the **go to** block.

If we were to replace our resetting block with this new block, we would see Frog glide to his position instead of just appearing there. The time it would take to "glide" depends on the number you input into this block.

See also

► To see more about the resetting aspects of the program, refer to the previous recipe, *Basic broadcasting and receiving*

► The next recipe, *Other fun graphic effects*, takes a look at other cool graphical effects we can incorporate into telling a story

Other fun graphic effects

Now that we have a lot of the other story-creating features, we can have a little fun changing graphics in our story! You might have already taken a look and played around with some of the **Looks** blocks we haven't really talked about yet. This is where we will formally look at a few more of these.

Getting ready

Here in this recipe, we're going to focus on changing the color effect. Later, we'll also see a few other things you can do with the appearance of sprites. Our time will be spent adding the following three blocks to what we have so far:

The first of these will help us give our sprites some fun effects while the other two will be used to reset those effects back to our starting place.

How to do it...

Let's get started:

1. Let's begin by making sure that everything is reset at the start of the program, even though we know nothing has been changed yet. This will make sure we don't forget to have our graphic effects reset later.

 These graphic effects are sprite specific, meaning you need to reset them for each sprite you plan on —eventually changing the graphics for. We're only going to change Monkey Mike here, but you may wish to change more.

2. Ensure that you have the script area for Monkey Mike open.

3. Drag over a green -flag block.

4. Also, drag a **clear graphic effects** block. We can now feel safe and know that each time our program runs, any graphic effects we've added along the way will be set back to normal.

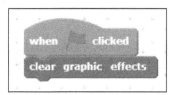

 You may not want to use the all-in-one block we just used. If you only change the color, use the second block that we mentioned here to only set the color effect back to 0. You can do this with any of the other graphic effects that are available too!

5. Next, we are going to delve into the realm of changing the color of a sprite. We don't have a way to merely select a specific color to change our sprite to. Instead, we change the value of the color effect.

6. Returning to our previous project, we'll make it so that Monkey Mike changes color when he is clicked. Drag over the **when this sprite clicked** block from the **Events** menu.

7. Returning to the **Looks** block menu, drag and connect the **change color effect by** block to the top hat block you just added.

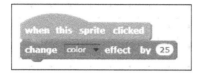

8. Depending on how extreme you want to make this change appear, adjust the number.

 Notice that you can adjust the number in the **change effect by** block by either a positive value or a negative value. A negative value will reverse any positive -value effect you've already applied. Play around with the numbers to see what happens!

9. You should now run your program and click on Monkey Mike several times to see the color effect change.

How it works...

In the background when you change the color effect, there are 200 possible color schemes available. This means if you input a value higher than 200, the actual color that will be displayed would be the equivalent of the number modulus 200. For example, if you input a color effect of 300, you will observe the same effect as you would get when you put in 100. Another example would be 450; this would be the same effect as 50.

There's more...

You may be interested in having more than one effect in your program. The good news is that not a whole lot changes beyond what we've just done!

Drag over an additional **change effect by** block to the script we've already been working on in this recipe.

Clicking on the drop-down arrow, as is shown in the previous screenshot, gives us all the other graphic effects that Scratch has included! Here is a brief description of what each does. Each of these also has a screenshot (with an effect value of 50 applied) as a reference to what it will do to your sprite.

Fisheye

You might recognize the fisheye effect from looking into a fish bowl at some point in your life. This effect makes the center of the image look distorted and somewhat rounded.

Whirl

Whirl adds a spiraling effect to your sprite. The higher the value, the more intense the spiral.

Pixelate

You've probably seen the pixelate effect before when you've zoomed in really close into a digital image. Images are made up of what are called pixels (small squares of color). The more pixels you fit into a small space, the sharper the image.

Mosaic

A mosaic image is made up of many images put together. This effect splits your image into a series of small copies of that image.

Brightness

This effect simply changes the brightness of your sprite. After a certain point, the brightness won't do much to your sprite.

Ghost

If you're looking for a good way to make it look like your sprite is disappearing, this is the effect for you! As you increase the value of this effect, your sprite will become more and more transparent until it eventually disappears.

Play around with these color effects. Depending on the story you are trying to tell, these can be really handy in giving your story some life.

See also

▶   If you'd like to see more on how you can use different color effects, they'll come up again, particularly in the *Graphic effects to backgrounds* recipe in *Chapter 3, Adding Animation*

3
Adding Animation

In this chapter, we will cover:

- ▶ Changing sprite costumes
- ▶ Switching backgrounds in a story
- ▶ Adding graphic effects to backgrounds
- ▶ Keyboard input to a program
- ▶ Getting the mouse position

Introduction

The previous chapter was focused on techniques you'll use in telling a story with Scratch. This chapter continues a lot of those ideas and will help us transit into the next chapter on basic gaming. Animation is a broad idea, here we don't mean just for stories, we also mean the types of animation you'll use with games, and anything else you do in Scratch.

Up until now, we've focused heavily on the Looks, Motion, Events, and Control blocks. We are still going to use a number of these blocks we've seen previously in the chapter, but now we'll focus much more on a new category; that is, the Sensing blocks. The Sensing blocks are helpful whenever you need to incorporate user interaction into your program or need sprites to abide by certain conditions. For instance, one of our recipes will involve getting your user to provide a keyboard response. You might also use the Sensing blocks to check if your sprite is touching something on the stage.

Before we dive into sensing, let's get acquainted with using what are called costumes.

Changing sprite costumes

You might be asking yourself right now what costumes are. One of the great things about programming with Scratch is that often the terms used match what they mean. A costume in Scratch is an appearance for your sprite. Think of it as dressing up your sprite to look like something else. You may have only worked with the default cat sprite, and believe it or not, there are costumes involved there too!

Getting ready

When you first load Scratch, you see the cat in the default costume, as shown in the following screenshot:

This cat can also take a different look though, which is shown in the following screenshot:

Having a second costume for our sprite can come in handy when we want to give our sprite the appearance of running (or maybe even dancing, as we'll see later in this recipe).

To get started, open up a new Scratch file.

How to do it...

The following are the steps we'll need for this recipe:

1. Notice that above the block palette, there are three tabs. The first of these we've been using all along to program our individual sprites. The second tab, which is in the same spot as the backdrop tab for the stage, is what we'll use to accomplish our goal here. Click on this area.

2. As we just saw, our default sprite comes with two costumes. If we click on the **Costumes** tab of our default sprite we'll see both of those costumes listed.

 Take note of how this area looks. It looks just like the background area when we changed backgrounds to the stage! This means we can import new costumes the same way we imported new backgrounds and the naming, deleting, and adjusting of these costumes works the same way.

You should see the following screenshot:

Now the key is just working with these costumes and making our sprite appear as if it is walking on the stage.

3. Now we'll make the sprite walk. Begin by returning to the **Scripts** tab of the default sprite. We are actually going to essentially take some programming from one of our past recipes and add more to it. You'll recognize parts of this as one of our very first recipes we completed in *Chapter 1, Getting Started with Scratch*.

4. Drag over the green flag block [when clicked] to the script area (from the **Events** category) for what is called Sprite1.

5. Place a **forever** loop directly underneath, from the **Control** category.

6. Inside this loop, place a **move () steps** block that can be found in the **Motion** category.

7. Change the number of steps our sprite moves from 10 to 2.

8. Also place the **if on edge, bounce** block from the **Motion** category.

 Recall when we changed the sprite settings in *Chapter 1, Getting Started with Scratch*, so our sprite only faces left or right. Apply that same setting here. This will make it so our sprite will not flip upside down on us when we make it walk.

Up until now, you should have the following block of code:

9. This code will make our sprite move across the stage, as we've done before. Now come the new parts. Take a look at the **Looks** category of blocks. The second set of these deal with costumes.

10. Click on the next costume block and drag it to the bottom of the **forever** loop we have.

11. If you click on the green flag, something shouldn't look right. Your sprite should be flickering as it moves across the stage. This is because we are changing costumes too quickly; perhaps this motion would look better if we made our sprite run across the stage.

12. To fix this, we'll need to use the technique we learned in *Chapter 2, Storytelling*, that is, using the **wait () secs** block in the **Control** category. Drag this block to the bottom of the loop and change the default to 0.5 seconds. Your sprite should now appear to be walking across the stage.

 Play around with the number of steps the sprite takes and the timing. This will give you practice with animation and seeing what looks right for your program.

Your final script should look like the following screenshot:

 The technique we used just now is actually very similar to animation that is done to **Graphics Interchange Format** (**GIF**) images. By incorporating frames similar to what we've done here with costumes, we can make animated pictures, you might have seen these before on the Internet! If you're interested, a quick search of the Web will turn up all kinds of results about GIF images.

How it works...

We only applied one true new block to this recipe, but let's take a moment to understand the logic of what is happening here.

Much of the logic works similarly to what we've done before. We click on the green flag to initiate the program. This triggers our script to start, which involves the **forever** loop. Everything that is contained in the **forever** loop continues until you stop the program manually.

Inside the **forever** loop we have four different blocks that make our cat walk across the stage, or at least appear to walk across (that is the beauty of animation, right?). Our sprite starts the first iteration of the loop by moving two steps, which would be equivalent of two pixels on the screen. If it hits the edge, it will bounce off, which will cause it to turn around—this is based on our setting from the sprite settings.

Our sprite's next costume is then triggered to take effect. This block looks for the next costume in our costume list, and then applies it.

 If you incorporate multiple costumes into a program, you'll want to take note of the order you have them in the list. If you don't, this block may have them appear at times you didn't plan for.

We then wait half a second, and the loop iterates again, repeating the same logic.

 Notice that we didn't ever add in a background to this recipe. Why not import the bench-with-view image from the Scratch library (under the **Outdoors** category)? With this image, your sprite will look like it's walking in the park!

There's more...

We have a couple of different ways with which we can differentiate and expand on this project. Let's take a look at them.

Making it dance

You might recall that at the beginning of this recipe we mentioned getting a character to dance. Let's take a moment to try that here. This can be a very effective technique in a story or game we create, or even just a good technique to better understand Scratch.

Create a new project, and delete the default sprite. Import a new sprite, in particular, choose the **People** category. You'll see several of these sprites have different appearances (notice in the following screenshot when **Cassy** is highlighted, it shows she has four costumes). Those are their various costumes created for you.

Choose the **Cassy** Dance pose to be your main sprite.

We now need to have the programming to make her dance (we'll worry about the costumes in a minute). Drag over the same blocks from the block palette as what we had for our default sprite in our last program, but without either of the motion blocks we used. You should see the following screenshot:

Now we are ready to get the costumes set up. Head over to the **Costumes** tab in the script area. Using the import feature (just as you would for backgrounds), import the three other costumes that are available. The costumes area should then look like the following screenshot. Note that if you are using Scratch 2.0, and working off of what we previously showed, this sprite already has four costumes imported for us!

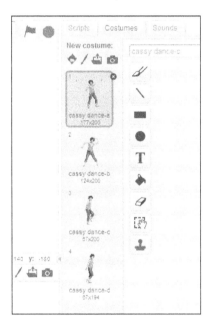

If you click on the green flag, you should see **Cassy** begin to dance. Depending on your preference, you may wish to move around the order of the costumes. Simply drag-and-drop them in the costume list to move the order.

Checking the costume number

For something like our break dancer program, or even more so with a program containing many more costumes, it may be beneficial to know while the program is running exactly which costume is currently in play.

Take a look at the **Looks** category. The third costume option, labeled **costume #**, has a check box next to it. Click on this box, you'll notice something pop up in the upper-left corner of the stage. This is the indicator for this particular sprite's costume, which in our case was called Cassy Dance.

The costume number is stored in Scratch as a variable. A variable is a way to store information. Scratch has several of these; you'll notice them as the rounded shaped blocks (like the ones in preceding screenshot). Later on, we'll place these rounded shape blocks in what are called operators. The check box indicates to Scratch that you wish to display the variable in the program. With any variable we work with we'll have this option.

This specific variable we are working with here is what is known as a local variable. A local variable is specific to one part of the program, and cannot be accessed by another object (such as another sprite). Later on, we'll see some instances of global variables, which are variables that can be accessed throughout the program.

Switching to a particular costume

We may desire to simply change to one specific costume in our costume list at some point. Notice in the screenshot we had of the costume list previously, we could change the names of the costumes. This is just like we could with backgrounds, sprites, and so on. You may find it useful to make this change yourself at some point.

In our **Looks** category of blocks, there is the switch to the **costume ()** block. You can drag this wherever you need to switch the costume and not go to the next one in the list. When using this block, the sprite will always change to that specific costume in the list.

See also

For this recipe we used a number of techniques from the previous two chapters that you may wish to read up on. Our next recipe will focus on what you might call the costumes of the stage, or backgrounds. Also take a look later in this chapter when we get to recipes on the **Sensing** block category.

Switching backgrounds in a story

This recipe is going to help us use similar tools within Scratch similar to what we used for changing costumes, to change the stage.

Getting ready

Let's continue with the program we used in the *There's more* section of the previous recipe with our dancing character.

To prepare for the programming we are about to do, go to the Stage script area and change the tab to **Backdrops**. Import several backgrounds that you'll want to change through during the time the break dancer is dancing. In the following screenshot, you'll notice we imported the first four that are available in the Outdoors folder, and deleted the default white background.

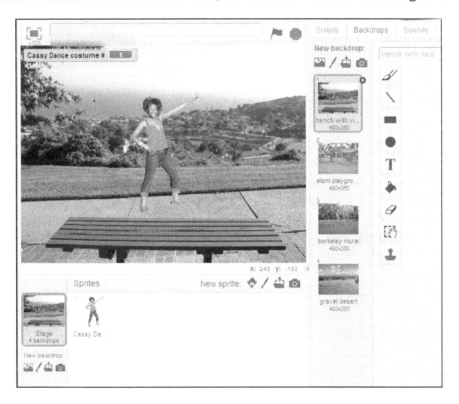

How to do it...

Let's get started. Perform the following steps:

1. Return to the **Scripts** tab of the script area for the stage. Also take a look at the block palette, particularly the **Looks** category of blocks. You'll see the first three are very similar (actually, nearly identical) to what we used in the last recipe. Our goal is to have the background change each time our dancer strikes a new pose. We'll drag over what could be deemed the stage equivalent to what we did in the last recipe.

2. First, we'll need the green flag block from **Events**.

3. Also insert a **forever** loop from **Control**.

4. Inside our **forever** loop, place the next backdrop block from the **Looks** category.

5. Also drop a **wait () secs** block underneath the block from step 4, and change the value to 0.5.

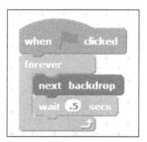

6. Next we'll run our script by clicking on the green flag. Each time your dancer is in a new position, the background will also change.

The background should change at the same time the costume changes, since we timed them that way, but keep in mind it may appear that there is an ever so slight amount of lag time present. This is normal based on the processing speed of the computer you are using. You might try using the broadcast and receive technique we used in *Chapter 2, Storytelling*, to minimize the lag time.

How it works...

Scratch is much like many other programming languages because it is object-oriented. This means we have various objects (in our case, sprites) that are created and have their own set of code. This is partially what allows us to have these simultaneous scripts running at the same time in Scratch.

Think of it this way, when you click on the green flag, both of these scripts; that is, the one for the stage as well as the one for our sprite, begin to play. We also have the two continuous forever loops that make our program continue on forever. You'll notice that much of the logic in this recipe is similar to the previous one, since in a sense we are using the same type of block.

 You might be wondering, or may have even noticed, what happens when the block we've used here (or the equivalent costume block) gets to the end of the list. The program simply starts over in the list from the top, it's that simple!

See also

Looking for a similar recipe to what we just worked on? Check out the first recipe, *Changing sprite costumes*, in this chapter. Also take a look at the next recipe where we'll investigate incorporating graphics effects to backgrounds.

Adding graphic effects to backgrounds

In *Chapter 2, Storytelling*, we explored adding a few different graphics effects to sprites. In this recipe, we are going to work on similar concepts with the background. This recipe will be similar to the last, in that we are implementing blocks that are very similar to what we've used in previous techniques.

Getting ready

Open a new Scratch project, and import a backdrop. If you want to mimic what we do here, we'll be using the desert background under the **Nature** category. We won't need to do anything with our sprite for this recipe, so the default cat is fine.

 As a good programming practice, delete the white background when you've imported a new one. If you don't plan on using something at all, it is good to keep it out of the program. This keeps your program clean (which makes it more efficient to run) and easier to read for others.

Ultimately in this recipe we're going to have the user press buttons on the stage to change the graphic effects of the background.

How to do it...

Let's get started by adding some buttons and making them work. The following steps will guide you:

1. To prepare our stage, we'll want to have some buttons. When we create buttons in Scratch, we'll create them as sprites. Import a new sprite. Under the category **Things**, you'll see several types of buttons.

2. Import the regular button, **Button3**.

3. You now have a button on the stage. You'll want to place it somewhere out of the way, so drag it down to the bottom.

4. Import another two buttons as well and drag them to the same area. All together, we should have three buttons when you are finished.

 You probably want to align your buttons as best you can. The important part here is that each button's **y** value in the coordinate plane be the same. Use the motion block that sets the **y** value to give all these the same value. For example, we used -134 in this recipe.

5. Let's take a moment to name all of our sprites so they'll be easy to recognize when we work with them. Under the sprite settings in the script area for each sprite, change the names. You can see the names we used in the following screenshot:

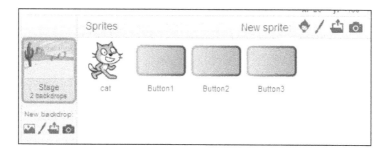

We now need to make these buttons different from each other, then we can program them to do what we want.

6. Start with **Button1** and go to the **Oostumes** tab of the script area. We'll see the paint editor.

7. Click on the **Text** tool (shown in the following screenshot) and type the word Reset.

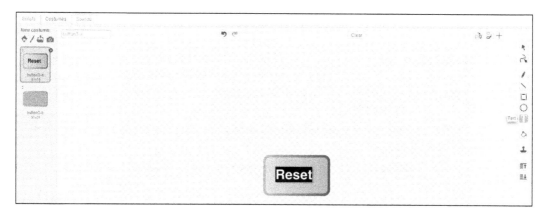

8. Change the font size so it will fit within the button, and move the text onto the button.

You now have a **Reset** button on your stage! Of course, it will not reset anything until we give it some script.

9. You'll want to now repeat the process for adding text to change the other two buttons. Give **Button2** the text `Add` and **Button3** the text `Minus`. Your stage should ultimately look pretty close to this:

10. Now our task becomes to make our buttons do something when clicked on. Since we are making all of our buttons do things to the background, we'll have to use the broadcast and receive techniques we've talked about in *Chapter 2, Storytelling* to accomplish what we want.

11. Under the script area for **Button1**, drag over a **when this sprite clicked** block from the **Events** blocks.

12. Attach a **broadcast ()** block and create a new broadcast message. Give it the name `ResetAll`.

13. Do the same for each of the other two buttons:

    1. Make the message name for **Button2** as Add.

    2. Make the message name for **Button3** as Minus.

14. We are now set so a different message will be broadcasted for each button that is clicked on. We will now use the stage to receive these messages. Go to the stage script area and drag over three of the **when I receive ()** top hat blocks. Ultimately we will have three scripts on the stage, one for each of the broadcasts we just created. In other words, you should have a top hat block for each message that will be broadcasted.

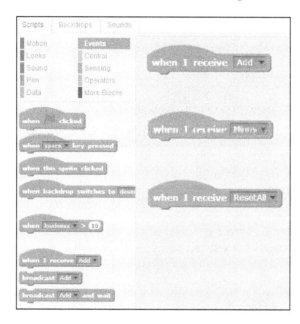

15. Open up the **Looks** category of blocks now. You'll notice that the last three deal with our graphics effects to the stage. Drag the last one, clear graphic effects, underneath the block dealing with **ResetAll**.

16. Next drag over a **change ()** effect to each of the other two blocks. Choose an effect and set it for both, ours will be **color**. Leave the script dealing with **Add** as 25, but change the script dealing with **Minus** to -25.

    The final script should look similar to the following screenshot:

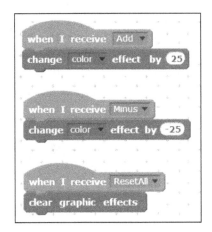

17. Now click on each of the buttons to test them. This is the first program you've created that doesn't require the green flag to be clicked on! Congratulations!

 Something to note is that when clicking too quickly, it registers as a double click and thus opens the script area of the button without applying the effect.

How it works...

So now let's understand what is happening. First off, why do we have to use so many broadcast and receive blocks? The answer to this is simple. Recall that the **when () clicked** block applies only to the sprite you are programming. We need something with another sprite to happen though we click on our sprite, so this technique allows us to do just that. The primary point to the broadcast and receive blocks is that it allows communication between sprites, as well as between sprites and the stage.

The programming logic of what we did here isn't too complicated, either. It all starts with our buttons. When we press the **Reset** button, the button broadcasts a message out to the rest of the program. We have the stage set so when it receives that message it clears all of the graphic effects that have been applied.

Note that instead of resetting all of the graphic effects, we could have alternatively used the other available button that sets the specific effect to a specific value to reset back to 0. This is a great idea if you are only working with one effect. If you want to reset all at once though, do what we did here. Moreover, you could use the alternative block to make your reset point something other than 0.

Button2 broadcasts a new message, as does **Button3**. When the stage receives what **Button2** has signaled, it increases the effect applied to the background. In our case, we set it to change the color. We could have, however, chosen any effect that we had from *Chapter 2, Storytelling*, when we dealt with graphic effects to sprites.

Button3 sends a signal that results in the exact opposite of what **Button2** does. In a sense, this makes both of these buttons undo buttons for each other.

There's more...

Here are a few additional tricks of the trade you might want to know.

A finished message

Let's add another layer to this program that gives us a response when we've finished making our changes. We'll design the program such that the cat will tell us when the graphic change has been finished.

To the end of each script on the stage, append a **broadcast** block. Give it a new message, call the message Done. Your script for the stage will then become as shown in the following screenshot:

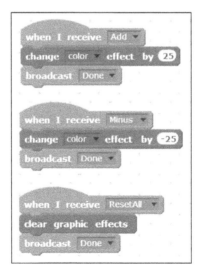

Now head over to the script area for our sprite called cat. Bring in a **when I receive()** block, and select the message to be the one you just created, **Done**. Attach to this a **say () for () secs** block and change the wording to say `Finished changing the graphics`.

The code for our cat is as shown in the following screenshot:

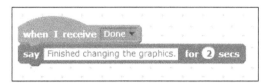

Now click on some of the buttons. Your cat should respond after you have clicked on a button, alerting you that the process is finished.

 Broadcasting a message when finished can be a useful technique, in particular when you have a script occur that does not have obvious results. Perhaps if you are doing some background calculations, or something else that you cannot see the result of, this confirmation can tell you when the program has finished.

We see our final stage as follows, with some changed color as our cat alerts us:

Adding other effects

We certainly don't have to restrict ourselves to just the color effect. You may wish to change the whirl effect. This is a simple change! Just return to the stage, and change the effect in both our **Add** and **Minus** scripts to something else, such as whirl.

You can also get creative with the buttons you show and have them do other things. We'll certainly get into more of that later!

Animating the button

You've probably noticed in a lot of programs you use on your computer that buttons often appear to be pressed when you click on them. We can give that same effect to our buttons in Scratch too!

Under each button, return to the **Costumes** tab of the script area. You'll notice a second button costume is available and already imported. That is meant to be a second costume to our button.

 You may want to add wording to the new costume for each button we just added, the same way we did for the original button. This is not necessary, but can add a nice touch.

We'll now need to adjust our script for each button to change the costume on each click.

We still want the first response to be the broadcast, so attach underneath this the **switch costume to** block that we've used before. Make sure **button3-b** is displayed in the block. Now add a **wait () secs** block. You can leave this as 1 second. Also add a **switch costume to ()** block at the end again. This time, have the block show **button3-a**.

The code for all of our buttons will then look similar to the following screenshot (with the **broadcast** command varying for each button, of course):

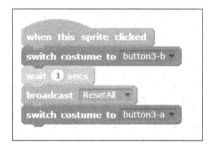

Make these changes to each of the other buttons. Try clicking on them. You should see the button appear to be pressed for 1 second.

See also

This recipe focused on changing graphic effects of the stage. You may want to see the section in *Chapter 2, Storytelling,* where we discussed changing the graphic effects to sprites as well. Additionally, checking out the recipe in *Chapter 2, Storytelling,* dealing with broadcasting and receiving could be beneficial since we used a lot of broadcasting and receiving in this recipe.

To start seeing how we can get more user interaction into our programs, take a look at the next recipe on *Keyboard input to a program.*

Keyboard input to a program

There are many cases where you may want to get your user to input some text or numbers into a program you are creating. For instance, you may want to get your program to get a value to change something from the user. You may also be playing a game and need input from the user to answer a question.

In this recipe, we'll explore how we can use a **Sensing** block that will accomplish all of this for us.

Getting ready

To prepare, let's create a new program. We'll create a program that creates a bit of user interaction and incorporates some of what we've learned already. Import a sprite of your choice, as well as a background of your choice, before we get going.

> We are using Tera (from Fantasy) as our sprite with bedroom2 (from Indoors) as our background. The rest of this section of the recipe is preparing for a couple of the optional things we'll do in this recipe.

How to do it...

The following are the steps for this recipe:

1. Drag over the when green flag clicked block from **Events**.

2. Attach a **say () for () secs** block and a **think () for () secs** block, both from **Looks**.

3. Program your character to say Hello!, and make it last for 2 seconds (both of these should be the default). Also program your sprite to think Hmm...I'll ask some questions, and repeat the answer for you. for 2 seconds.

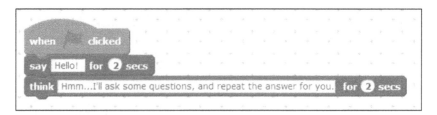

4. Change the block palette to the Sensing options. You'll notice two blocks we can use towards the top of the list, as shown in the following screenshot:

The first of these blocks prompts a question to the user, as well as an area to input that question via the keyboard. The second one of these is a local variable that contains the input from the user. More on variables can be found later in this chapter.

5. Drag over the **ask () and wait** block but don't change the default text. We want the first question asked to be the user's name.

6. Also drag over another **say () for () secs** block from **Looks**.

7. Now, place the **answer** block from **Sensing** in the place where you would normally place the text for the **say** block you just dragged over.

8. Also drag over another **ask** block from **Sensing**. This time change the text to say What is your favorite color?

9. Drag over yet another **say** block. Just as we did before, place the **answer** block inside of this. Your code so far should be as follows:

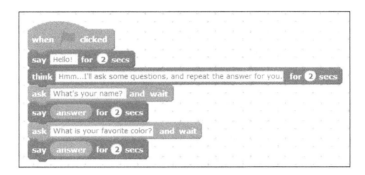

The prompt you'll see should look something like this when you run the program with the green flag:

10. The user can click on either the check mark shown, or hit *Enter* on the keyboard, when they are done typing.

Notice that we used the same variable for both of these. That's because this variable is changed automatically when we answer a new question. Be careful when using this block to not overwrite input before you are done using it! Later on, we'll find a safer way to store our variables so we don't have to worry quite as much.

11. We're now going to add to the end of this a series of costume changes, determined by the user. Add another **ask** block and have it ask the user How many times do you want me to change my facial expression?

12. We're going to have the costume change an appropriate number of times based on what the user types. Under the **Control** blocks, drag over a **repeat** loop.

13. Instead of typing a number into the loop, drag over the **answer** block as we've been doing with the **say** blocks (from the **Sensing** category).

14. Inside the loop place a **next costume** block from the **Looks** category.

15. Add in a **wait () secs** block from **Control**. Change the time to 0.5.

16. Now try running your program. If you input 16 into the last question, you should see your character change costumes 16 times. For your reference, the final code is as follows:

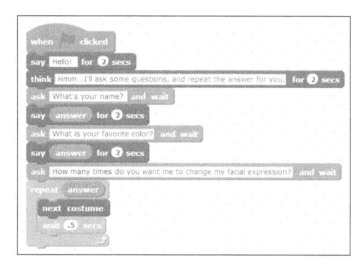

If we were making our character dance, you might want to have one **next costume** block and one **wait** block for each costume you have. This means that when you input the number 2 to dance 2 times, it doesn't just look like one dance.

How it works...

So now you ask, what is the key to what is going on here? We simply need to understand the **ask** block, much of the rest stems from what we've done before!

As we've mentioned, the **ask** block prompts the user for some input. This input can be anything you want, text or a number. Scratch automatically tells how it should use what is given based on the way you code the answer.

For instance, we placed the **answer** block somewhere text was needed, so Scratch simply used the answer as text. It can be problematic if you cannot discover if input is a number or text. It would even do this if you input a number when asked for a name or color. When we placed the answer block where a number was needed, Scratch tries to use the input as a number. In the event the answer given was not a number the loop would simply not run, it would just move to the next part of the code (if there was any) and we would observe no costume changes.

There's more...

Let's work a bit more with variables for a moment.

Using better defined variables

In our recipe so far we saw the use of the local variable represented by the **answer** block. Now is a good time to talk about other variables that can be used in Scratch, in particular, the ones you create yourself. If we're worried about one of these inputs from the keyboard being overwritten, this would be the case where we'd want to create a new variable.

What we'll do to illustrate this idea is head over to the last category listed in the block palette, **Data**. We'll use these in future programs, so now is a good time to get an introduction. In this category you should see two options, they are **Make a variable** and **Make a list**. A variable is just a place to store a simple bit of information, like a number. A list is a series of related bits of information, much like when you make a to-do list or a shopping list.

Click on the **Make a variable** button. A dialog box will appear asking for a variable name. Type in loopNumber, as shown in the following screenshot, and leave it applicable for all sprites.

Recall what we said before about local variables and global variable. When Scratch asks you about applying this variable to all sprites versus for this sprite only, it is asking if you want to create a local (for this sprite only) or global (for all sprites) variable. Note that a global variable is accessible by all sprites and the background so you can communicate between them. This can be very powerful when used in combination with the **broadcast** command. With Scratch 2.0, we can now create what are called Cloud variables, which are stored on the Scratch server and can be used between programs we create.

After you've created the variable, a whole group of new blocks will appear in the **Data** category. It should look like the following screenshot:

The first of these is similar to the **answer** block that we used to get the value for our program. Notice the check box next to the variable. This is very important when you are building programs. It shows your variable on the stage so you can see the value while you are programming. Once everything is working, uncheck the box so it is no longer shown on the stage.

The second one, **set () to ()**, is what defines the variable and sets it to a certain value. Remember what we said in the previous chapter about resetting each time the program starts? We'll want to do that with variables too.

Change () by () can be used to either increase or decrease your variable. The last two aid in displaying the variable, or hiding it during the course of your program.

One thing we may want to do is adjust our program so we can use the last answer more times if we need to, but it still allows us to ask more questions. Drag over the **set () to ()** block to just above the **repeat** loop. Now, move the **answer** block out of the loop and into the spot where we have 0 now for our variable. See the following screenshot:

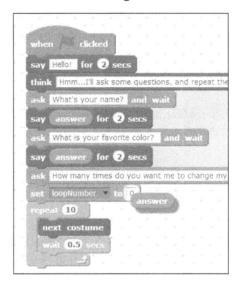

This means after the question is asked, the variable is set to whatever was input through the keyboard.

Lastly, drag over the **loopNumber** block representing that specific variable to where we just took the **answer** block from in the **repeat** loop. Your final code should look like the following screenshot:

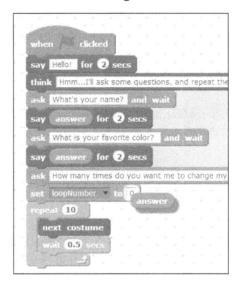

Nothing will change in how this program runs, but now if we extend it, we can use the **ask** and **answer** blocks without worrying about losing the number that was input. We'll have that stored as **loopNumber** until we change it in the program.

See also

This was your first introduction to some of the **Sensing** blocks as well as variables. Take a look at the last recipe to see how to incorporate buttons into your program. In the next recipe, we'll focus on getting the mouse position and incorporating it into the program.

Getting the mouse position

There are many times where it may be useful to have the mouse position in the program. Perhaps you want an object to follow the mouse, perhaps you want something to happen based on the mouse position, such as a graphic effect.

Getting ready

In this recipe, we're going to create a program that makes our sprite change its graphic effects based on the mouse position.

Start off by creating a new file and importing a new sprite. In our case, we've imported **Monkey1** with the white background.

How to do it...

We're going to apply two effects, one based on the mouse's horizontal direction, another based on the mouse's vertical direction. Follow along with these steps:

1. Drag over a green flag block (from **Events**).
2. Drag over a **forever** loop (from **Control**).
3. Inside the **forever** loop, drop a **set () effect to ()** block from the **Looks** category and make the effect that we work with whirl.

4. Also into the **forever** loop, drop a **set () effect to ()** block as well, this time make the effect **color**. We now have something similar to the following screenshot:

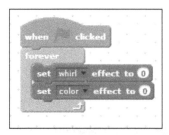

5. Now to introduce our new block from the **Sensing** category, change the focus over to the **Sensing** blocks. You'll see three mouse related blocks, shown in the following screenshot:

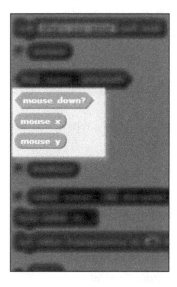

The first block returns either true or false to the program. True if the mouse button is currently being held down, false if the mouse button is not being held down. We'll try using this block a bit later.

The second two return information on the mouse position, one for the mouse position x-value, the other for the mouse position y-value.

6. Drag over the **mouse y** block into **set () effect to ()** we set up for **color**.

7. Drag the **mouse x** block into **set () effect to ()** we set up for the **whirl** effect. The final code is as shown in the following screenshot:

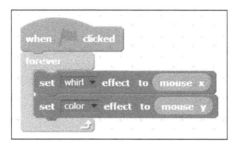

8. Click on the green flag and move your mouse around the screen. You should see both the color and amount of whirl change based on where you move your mouse!

How it works...

This recipe makes use of two new blocks we haven't seen before, both from **Sensing**. What we have happening in this program is based on us clicking on the green flag. Upon clicking on the green flag, both scripts run simultaneously, as we've learned before.

The **forever** loop means the same thing constantly keeps happening. In each case, the mouse position is found. This is returned as a number, different for each the x-value and y-value. Our program then uses that number to set the value for the appropriate effect.

Really, we could use these two blocks to get the mouse position and return it anywhere we need a number. This could also be useful in such things as making a game, which we'll get to in the next chapter.

There's more...

What about that third block we mentioned before? How could we use that one?

Let's make our sprite disappear whenever we hold the left mouse button down. To do this, we'll need another when green flag clicked block, as well as another forever loop. This time, drop in the loop a new block from the **Control** category called the **if () then else** block, seen in the following screenshot:

This block allows us to define a condition to look for, but also define what happens when that condition is not met. Return to the **Sensing** category and drag the **mouse down?** block into the condition spot (the small hexagon) next to the word **if** in the block. Then drag a **set () effect to ()** block into each open spot in our if else block we just dragged over. Change the effect to **ghost**.

For the first of the effect changing blocks, make the value 200. For the second, leave it as 0. This way, when we click on the mouse, the **if** statement becomes true, and the ghost effect becomes 200. Once we let go of the mouse button the ghost effect returns to 0.

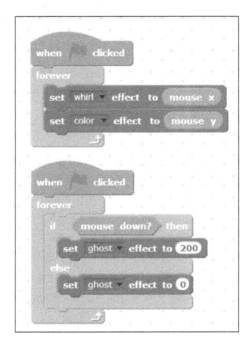

Test it out! Your sprite should still change color and disappear when you click on the mouse button!

4

Basic Gaming

In this chapter, we will cover:

- ▸ Creating a moving object
- ▸ Adding another ball
- ▸ Object interaction with a background
- ▸ User interaction with a game
- ▸ Using mouse control
- ▸ Keeping score
- ▸ Objects disappearing
- ▸ Building a maze
- ▸ Using the timer

Introduction

Up until this chapter, we've used Scratch to either build the foundation for a game or tell a story. Our last chapter was focused on adding animation and developing other fundamentals that we needed to get going in this chapter. We're going to focus on several Scratch principles here, including working more heavily with variables, digging deeper into sensing blocks, and continuing with looks and motion blocks we've used before. Now we're going to turn our attention to building our very first couple of games!

Before we can get into anything too advanced we need to build some basic games. Our very first game will be developed through a few recipes that will result in a ball bouncing across the stage that we need to prevent from hitting the left wall. The second game we create will be a maze game. Our goal will be to navigate through the maze from the start to the end.

Let's get started!

Creating a moving object

Our first recipe involves making a ball move across the stage for us to work with.

Getting ready

To get this recipe going, we don't need to worry about adding a background like we've done in the past. This recipe doesn't have much in terms of prerequisites.

First, delete the default sprite from the stage. We'll now need to import a ball to use for bouncing. Import a new sprite. Under the **Things** category you'll notice a few choices. Select the one you want to use. We used a beach ball, but the choice is yours. You can refer to *Chapter 1, Getting Started with Scratch* if you can't quite remember how to do this.

> When importing the sprite, you'll see a version of the beach ball that indicates there are scripts already attached to it—it is named bouncy ball. We don't want to use that one here, but this is a quick way to import a sprite that has a bouncing function built into it already.

For the sake of good naming, change the name of the sprite from `Sprite1` to `Ball1`. Depending on the sprite you chose, the default name may already be different.

How to do it...

Our goal is to make the ball we've just imported bounce (similar to how a ball in real life would move) around the screen. Here's how we take care of that task:

1. Drag over the ▢ block to the script area for the ball.
2. Attach a **forever** loop to this block.
3. Bring in a **move () steps** block to the sequence inside the **forever** loop.
4. Also, place an **if on edge, bounce** block within the loop.
5. Lastly, drag over a **turn () degrees** block into the forever loop.
6. Continuing from step 5, change the value of this new block to 1 degree instead of 15.

> Do you recall, we did a similar program before? We want to make sure this time we do not change the sprite settings to have the ball only face left and right. Now is a case where we want the ball to bounce all over the screen.

7. Test out your preliminary game by clicking on the green flag. Your ball should begin moving all around the stage.

8. You might notice that it is moving rather quickly. Play around with the number in the **move () steps** block to take care of this issue. We'll stick with five steps for our version.

Your final code should look like this:

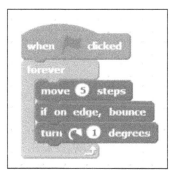

How it works...

This recipe, in essence is very similar to what we've done in the previous chapters, except that now we're getting ready to apply it to a new situation—a game.

When we click on the green flag, the **forever** loop is activated. This begins an infinite cycle of running the code that is contained within the loop. First, the ball is moved five steps (which we recall is five pixels on the screen). Then, the program checks to see if the ball is at the edge of the stage. If it is, the ball will bounce off into the other direction. If it is not, nothing changes and the next block runs.

Next comes our new block that we haven't used before. The **turn () degrees** block is used to rotate our sprites within the program. It would be quite a boring game if the ball just went back and forth in the same direction, wouldn't it? To avoid this, we have the ball change the angle it's moving towards by a slight amount (1 degree) after each iteration of the loop.

The result is a ball moving around the screen that we can now work with!

Another important couple of notes on Scratch are on a couple of types of blocks we have. Note that **reporter blocks**—those blocks with rounded corners—and **Boolean blocks**—those that hold conditions—are very different. Our reporter blocks contain variables, user entered text, and so on. We can place these within blocks in Scratch that take an input. Our Boolean blocks return either true or false, so might be used when verifying when something is occurring.

There's more...

What if we wanted to make this a really complicated game? We might be able to accomplish this in two ways, one simple way first. The second way is coming up in our next recipe.

The simple way

Simply change the value in the **move () steps** block. If you increase this value, the ball will move faster, which will make it hard to follow.

You might also consider changing the number of degrees the ball rotates in the loop. This will result in the ball rotating around the screen in a more unpredictable fashion.

 Don't make the degree value too high. Doing so may result in the ball essentially just spinning in place, which defeats the goal you were trying to attain.

Adding another ball

A second, and slightly more complex way, of making your game more challenging would be to incorporate another moving ball into the mix. Let's do that here.

Getting ready

To prepare for this, import another ball sprite, perhaps the basketball or baseball. Give this new ball the same script that you gave to the first ball. Also name this ball `Ball2` instead of `Sprite1`.

Both balls will now bounce around the screen, but will seemingly do nothing special when they touch. Now the challenge becomes to make these balls bounce off of each other.

How to do it...

To accomplish this task, start with either sprite's script area. Ultimately, we'll add the same script to the other sprite too.

 Note that you can right-click on a sprite and click on Duplicate to save time.

1. Drag over a second green flag block.

   Thus we're starting another sequence of code.

2. Drag a **forever** block underneath the previous block.

3. Inside our **forever** loop, drag an **if () then** block, also from the **Control** category.

4. Inside the conditional area to the **forever** loop you just placed in the code, from the sensing blocks drag in a **touching ()?** block. Use the drop-down menu in this new sensing block to select the other sprite.

5. Inside this new loop, drag a **turn () degrees** block, the same one we used in the previous recipe and set the value to 180.

6. Drag a **move () steps** block into the loop from **Motion**. Set the value to 100.

7. Now copy over the same script; the only difference should be that the sensing block should read the opposite sprite.

Here is an example of what it should look like all together:

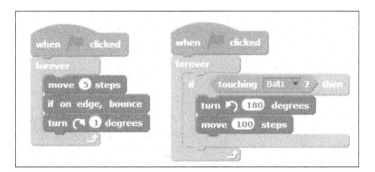

How it works...

Once we click on the green flag block, both sequences of code start at the same time. Let's examine just our second set of code.

After clicking on the green flag block, a conditional **forever** loop begins. This means that the code within the loop will continue to be repeated until the condition is not true. In the case of this game, this loop will not actually be running most of the time. Instead, it will just be waiting idle to run until the condition is met.

The condition we imposed is that the two sprites should touch. As we added the same code to each sprite, the same thing will happen to each sprite when the condition is met. Ultimately, our **turn () degrees** block will cause each ball to change and head in the opposite direction. Our **move () steps** block will help to keep the balls apart. This will give them the appearance of bouncing off of each other when they touch, which makes them more lifelike.

There's more...

This recipe leaves open the opportunity for a whole extra game that we're not creating here! If you continue to import more sprites similar to how we've done, you can make a game where the challenge is to click on the balls to make them disappear. The object of the game would then be to clear the stage.

We'll take a look at making the balls disappear in a later recipe in this chapter.

See also

▶ The *Objects disappearing* recipe

Object interaction with a background

We are going to want to make something separate happen when the balls touch the left boundary of the stage. This may mean a loss in points; however, for the time being we'll just make it end the game.

Getting ready

We'll first turn our attention to the stage. More specifically, we need to adjust our white background. Our goal is to find a way to differentiate the left boundary of the stage from the rest of the stage.

Get this started by going to the **Backdrops** tab of the stage script area. There we see our default white background. We'll also see the **Paint Editor**.

You will notice the rectangle tool on the side. Click on that and make a thin line moving from the top of the stage to the bottom on the left. Refer to the following screenshot for a guideline. Make sure you make the line thick enough so that it will be detected with the blocks we are about to add:

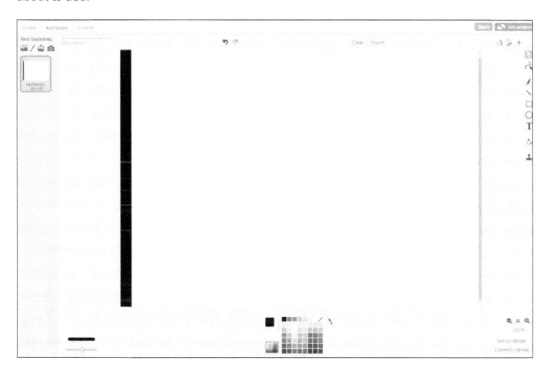

We're ready to go!

How to do it...

Return to the script area for either ball and perform the following steps:

1. We'll need to create a third script in our script area to handle this goal. To get started, drag over another 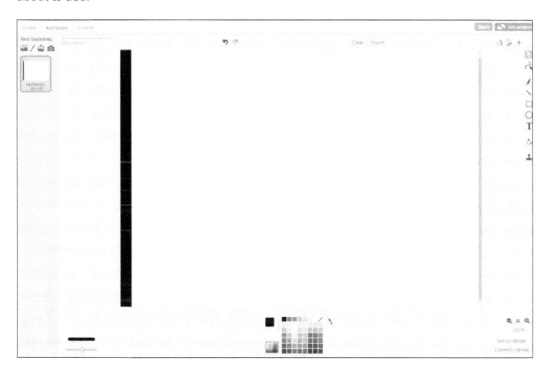 block.

2. Drag over a **forever** loop as we did in the previous recipe.

3. Drag in an **if () then** block.

4. In the conditional area of the loop we just created, head over to the **Sensing** blocks. Drag over the **touching color ()?** block.

5. Click on the small block of color within the block you just dragged over; your cursor should change to a different icon. Click on the black line you created on the stage. The block of color will change to the same color as the one you clicked on using the tool.

6. Now return to the **Control** blocks. At the end of the list is the **stop all** block. Drag this within the loop we've added.

7. Lastly, copy the same set of code over to the other sprite. You should have the following code in each sprite, in addition to what we have from previous recipes:

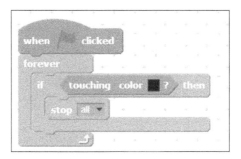

How it works...

Again with this recipe, we begin with the green flag block to get things going. Collectively, we now have three scripts running for each sprite, which means a total of six scripts running simultaneously when we click on the green flag.

The important thing to note that is different with this set of code as opposed to our last recipe is the new **touching color ()?** block. This block is another **Sensing** one, similar to what we used in the last recipe. This block fills in for a place where we need a condition to be checked, such as in our **forever if** loop. We see that whenever the sprite is touching the color black, the condition is true and the script within the **forever if** loop runs. In this case, the script is the **stop all** block.

The stop all block is a new block we haven't used before. It is essentially an **end-all** block that **stops all** scripts in the program from running.

If you press the green flag and run the program, you'll probably notice that the game won't last long. In fact, as soon as one of the balls hits the left boundary, the game will end. We'll find a way to make our game a bit more interesting in the next recipe.

There's more...

Until we can make something more exciting happen in the next recipe, instead of using the **stop all** block, we could simply have our program acknowledge that a ball has hit the boundary.

To do this, remove the **stop all** block. Check out the **Looks** blocks and drag in **say () for () secs** that we've used before. Change the text to say something like I've hit the wall!. Now if you run the program, when the ball touches the boundary on the left, it will appear as if the sprite is speaking and mentioning that it has touched the boundary. Remember to add the **stop all** block to both balls if you want them to both behave the same way.

▸ For more information on adding scoring to this game, refer to the *Keeping score* recipe. If you need a refresher on how to use a few of the blocks we've used in this recipe, refer to *Chapter 1, Getting Started with Scratch* and *Chapter 2, Storytelling*.

User interaction with a game

One of the main requirements for most games, or at least the good ones, is that there exists some sort of user interaction. Here, we'll create a new sprite that moves up and down on the boundary we created. This will prevent the balls from hitting the boundary, and thus creates a basic game for us. This is similar to the classic 'pong' bat and ball game, one of the earliest video games ever created.

Getting ready

We first need a sprite that will be controlled by the user. Under the stage, near where we select to import a new sprite, click on the second button to paint a new sprite.

The familiar **Paint Editor** dialog box will appear. Click on the same rectangular tool we used before and change the color (we're going to use red). Draw a small rectangle in the middle of the screen, similar to the following screenshot:

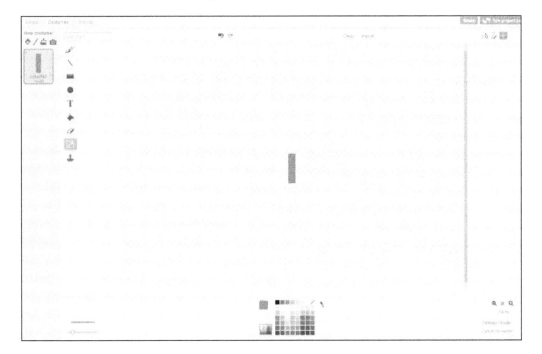

Notice the three buttons in the upper-right corner?

It is critical that you use the third button to mark the center of your box you just created.

The new sprite will appear in the middle of the stage. Change the name of the sprite to `userBar`. Drag it to the center of the boundary, as shown in the following screenshot:

 If you can't recall how to change the name of a sprite, head back to the *Special Sprite Settings* recipe of *Chapter 1, Getting started with scratch.*

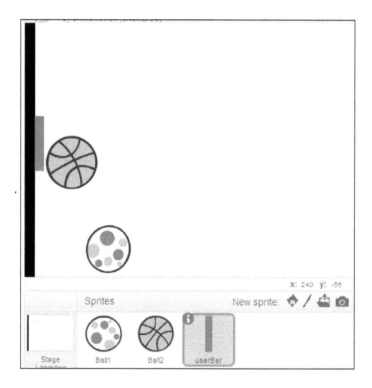

This will be the starting point for our red bar.

How to do it...

We ultimately want the red bar to move up and down, at the whim of the user to block the balls from hitting the boundary. This is how we accomplish it:

1. In the script area of `userBar`, drag over a 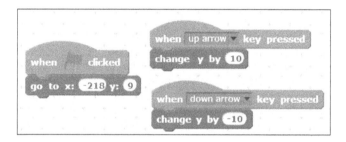 block.

2. Underneath this block, return to **Motion** and drag over a **go to x: () y: ()** block.

3. We now need two other scripts. Drag over a **when () key pressed** block from **Events**. This is another top hat block so nothing attaches to the top of it.

4. Change the key to **up arrow** by selecting it from the drop-down menu of the block.

5. Return to the **Motion** block. Drag over a **change y by ()** block and attach it to the top hat block we just added. Leave the value at `10`.

6. Now do the same thing with another set of scripts for **down arrow**. This time though, you'll want to make the value `-10`.

You should now have the following:

Try pressing the up and down arrows on your keyboard; you should see the red bar move up and down!

Now we just need to get the balls bouncing off of the bar. This is actually similar to what we've done already in this chapter!

1. Drag over a block to one of the ball sprites.

2. Attach to this a **forever** loop.

3. Within the loop, drag an **if () then** block from **Control**.

4. For the condition, drag over a **touching color ()?** block from the **Sensing** category.

5. Change the color to the shade of red used in `userBar`. Recall that you do this by clicking on the box of color and clicking on the color you want.

6. Inside of the **forever** loop, drag the **turn () degrees** block. Set this to `180` degrees.

Create (or copy) the same script to the other ball you have.

Test out your game! You should now be able to control the red bar using your keyboard, and keep the balls from hitting the boundary.

 You may want to play around with the speed at which the bar moves; 10 steps may be a little difficult to keep the game going for a while. It's your game, so it's all up to you!

A sample code for one of the balls would be:

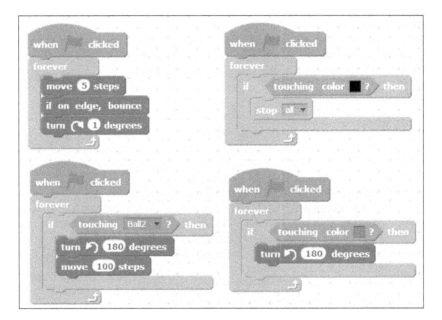

How it works...

Now the question arises, "What's going on here?"

This is probably the most complex program we've created so far, so it's worth looking at. The main change from what we had done in the last recipe is the control of the red bar as well as the balls bouncing off of the red bar.

If we look at the script for the red bar, we have two important scripts that control the movement of the bar. Movement upwards and movement downwards are two independent controls. We have a top hat block, which acts as a listener, that is activated when we press the up arrow. In technical terms, the block is listening for an event (hence, the category of blocks being called **Events**). We also have one for the down arrow. Once we press the respective key, the code beneath it begins to run.

We actually don't have anything complicated attached to these two blocks, either. We simply have a **Motion** block that changes the y-value in the coordinate plane on the stage. If we press the up arrow, it moves in the positive direction (up), and if we press the down arrow, it moves in the negative direction (down).

In terms of the balls bouncing off of the red bar, this is essentially the same as what we accomplished in a few of the previous recipes in this chapter. The conditional **forever** loop is activated when the ball is touching the color red. From there, the ball rotates in the other direction and moves away from the boundary.

> You may want to be careful selecting colors to use. For instance, notice that we used two different colors for the boundary and `userBar`. If these were the same color, this would not work. The same thing applies if we have the color black used elsewhere in the game.

Using mouse control

Alternatively, we could use the mouse to control the red bar and give the mouse the freedom to move all around the stage.

Here's how we could go about doing this.

Getting ready

To get started, we'll need to take our program from the end of the last recipe and eliminate the arrow key controls; this way we can focus on the mouse controls.

In the `userBar` sprite, delete all three scripts that we have. Now we're ready to go!

How to do it...

1. Drag over a block to the script area for `userBar`.
2. Insert a **forever** loop below the top hat block we just placed.

3. Inside the forever loop, place a **go to ()** block from the **Motion** category.

4. Using the drop-down menu in the new block you just dragged over and select the **mouse-pointer** option.

Your code should look like the following set of blocks:

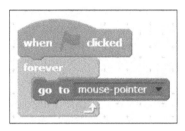

Now give playing your game a shot!

How it works...

The code for this recipe is much simpler than our last recipe. It starts when we have the green flag clicked, which initiates a **forever** loop. From there, the program is constantly sending the red bar to wherever the mouse pointer is on the stage.

We then still have our original code we created, which makes the balls bounce off of the red bar. We now have a game that is a little easier to play and not controlled by the keyboard.

There's more...

You may want to consider making your game a bit more challenging now that we have decreased the difficulty. One way to do this would be to increase the speed of the balls. Recall that we can do this by changing the value of the **move () steps** block in the script area for each ball.

We may also want to consider having different speeds for each ball, which would add to the difficulty as well. This could be accomplished by using the **pick random () to ()** block from the **Operators** category.

Finally, you may wish to add more than two balls to the program. Multiples of these sprites, as shown in the following screenshot, might make the game a bit more complex to play:

An easy way to insert more of the ball sprites into the program is to right-click on the sprite you want to replicate and click on Duplicate. This way you don't have to recreate any code.

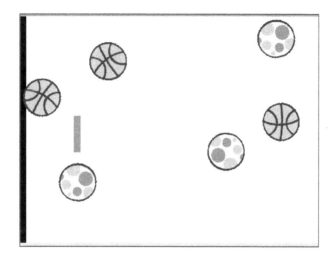

 Have you caught a flaw yet in the game? Notice that by adding more bouncy balls, we actually need to add more scripts to make the balls bounce off of each other. If we don't, they'll only be bouncing off of the original one we created!

Keeping score

Most good games have a mechanism built in to keep track of scoring. We're now going to take the game we've been working on and integrate some scoring.

We also have duplicated several of our sprites, so we now have six bouncing balls on the stage. You may choose to follow our lead, or you may not, that part is up to you.

The primary way we'll change the score in this game is by having the score increase by one point for each ball you successfully bounce. We know this leaves you open to the possibility to cheat in the game, but hey, this is the basic gaming section right?

Getting ready

For this recipe, you can use either the version of the game we created in the last recipe, or the version from the *User interaction with a game* recipe. We're going to use the version that has the mouse control involved, and not the one with arrow keys.

How to do it...

We'll start off by increasing our score by one point each time we hit a ball with the red bar.

To increase the score, perform the following steps:

1. Select the **Data** category of blocks (for any sprite).

2. Click on the button that says **Make a variable**.

3. Give the variable the name Score. Be sure that all sprites are checked, and then click on **OK**.

4. Go to the script area of the stage.

5. Drag over a  block and attach the **set () to ()** block below it that is now in the **Data** category.

6. Using the drop-down menu of the **Data** block **set () to ()**, **Score** should be the only option as we only created one variable. Also, leave the default value of **0** in the block.

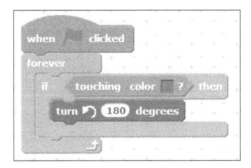

7. Return to the script area for any ball in your stage. We suggest you work your way left to right in the sprite list if you have multiple bouncing balls created.

8. We'll focus for a moment on the script that controls our ball bouncing off the red bar, as shown in the following screenshot:

9. Drag over the **change () by ()** block from the **Data** category. Place it under the **turn () degrees** block we have already. Notice again that **Score** is already in the block. We won't change the default value on this either.

10. Complete the same procedure for each ball you have in your program. You'll have something like this:

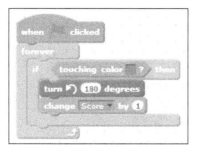

 If you've added more than two bouncing balls to your program as we have, you may find right now that it is hard to get the program running. We're about to complete a solution to that now.

Instead of having the game end when we touch the boundary, we'll have the game decrease the score. Perform the following steps to decrease the score:

1. Remove the **stop all** block from the scripts for each ball we have in the program.

2. Replace this script with the **change () by ()** block we used previously.

3. Make the value of this block -1.

How it works...

Now our game is set up to keep basic score. We've set it up in such a way that each time the red bar hits one of the bouncing balls, the score will be increased by one point. At the same time, if a ball touches our original boundary, the score will be decreased by one point.

 This game may actually work optimally with one or two bouncing balls. Adding more bouncing balls, as we've done here, may decrease the functionality of the game.

Objects disappearing

When we play the game we have created so far, we may want more to happen when the red bar hits a ball. Let's follow this recipe to make the ball disappear from the stage.

Getting ready

Continue with the game we've been making all along in this chapter. There isn't much we need to prepare, as long as you've been following the recipes up until now.

How to do it...

Apply the following to each bouncing ball sprite:

1. Under the **Looks** category, find the **hide** block. Drag this to our script that controls bouncing off of the red bar.
2. Under any of the green flag top hat blocks, drop a **show** block from the **Looks** category between the top hat block and the loop.

How it works...

By adding these two simple blocks we can make it so that each time the game starts, all of the bouncing balls are brought back on the stage. As soon as they touch the red bar, they will disappear for the remainder of the game.

You might notice, though, that the score will keep increasing. This is because those bouncing balls are still there, you just can't see them. To fix this you'll need to insert the following code after the **hide** command:

This will center the ball for the remainder of the game away from our red bar.

See also

▸   The *User interaction in a game*, *Using mouse control*, and *Keeping score* recipes

Building a maze

Now we'll begin creating a new game. This will be a maze game where the user moves a mouse around the stage and out of the maze.

Getting ready

We need to start off by constructing our stage. Enter the script area for the stage and edit the background as we've done in previous recipes. We have created a very basic maze as shown in the following screenshot. You can get as creative as you like.

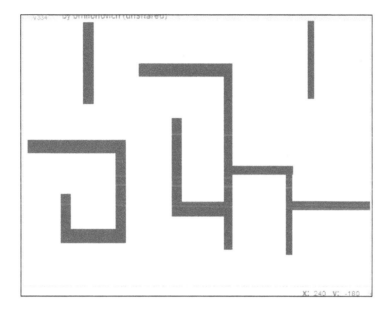

We will now need to decide on our sprite that will work its way through the maze, as well as a target.

Import a new sprite. Under the **Animals** category you'll see a mouse. Create the following set of code within the mouse script area:

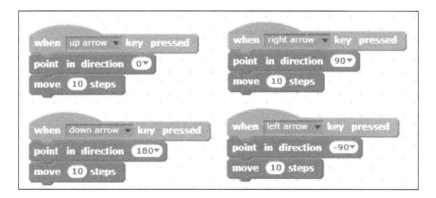

These scripts create movements based on the arrow keys being pressed on the keyboard. Shrink the mouse down by several sizes to make it fit well into your maze.

To make the target, paint a new sprite. Use the circle tool to create a green dot. Change the name to `Target` and center the sprite as we did earlier in this chapter. Place both of these in the positions you desire to start and end, ours are shown here:

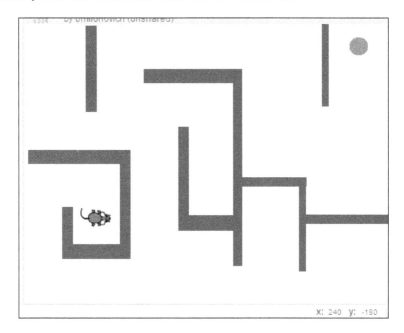

How to do it...

Now that we've gotten the maze designed, we just need to do a bit of programming to get it going.

Hitting the wall: This procedure will get us set up for how our mouse will react if we hit the wall of the maze.

1. In the script area for the mouse, drag over a **when clicked** block.

2. Attach to this a **go to x: () y: ()** block. The values of this will be your mouse's starting position.

3. Drag over a **forever** loop followed by an **if () then** block as we've used previously in this chapter.

4. Place a sensing condition in the loop's conditional requirement. We'll use the **touching color ()?** block. Set the color to be the color of the walls in your maze.

5. Inside the **forever** loop, drag a **say () for () secs** block. Leave the number of seconds set as the default. Change the text to say `I hit the wall!`.

6. Drag over a **go to x: () y: ()** block and attach it to the block we added in step 5. The values in this should match the values from the similar block we added in step 2.

Hitting the target: This set of procedures will notify us that we've hit the target.

1. Drag over a 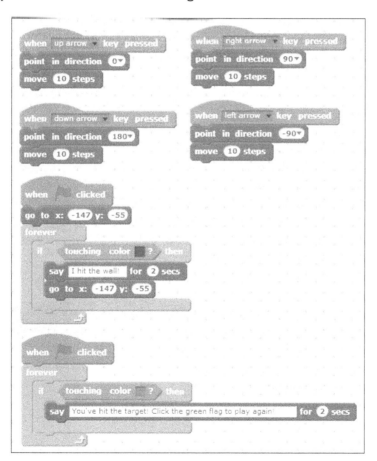 block.

2. Also, drag over a **forever** block followed by an **if () then** block as we did in the last procedure.

3. Use the same type of condition we did previously, this time making the color the shade of green we used in our target dot.

4. Insert a **say () for () secs** block with the text `You've hit the target! Click the green flag to play again!`.

The code for your mouse should look something like this now:

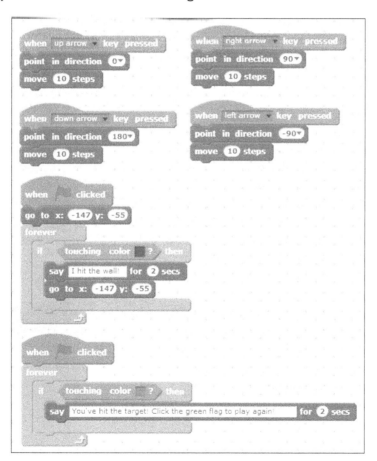

How it works...

We added two key pieces of code to this one. Each one is based on the mouse touching a specific color. The important thing to note is that we reset the mouse's position each time it hits the wall. If we were to not use the **go to x: () y: ()** block to do this, our mouse could roam around the stage wherever the user wanted to move it to.

 We had you create your target as a separate sprite from the stage, but we actually could have just had the color be built into the stage like the maze is built. This technique gives us the flexibility to move our target around the stage.

There's more...

An alternative for our method of hitting the target could be as follows. Instead of using the **touching color ()?** block that we used, we could have instead used the **touching ()?** block under the **Sensing** category. This would perform the same task, it's just another way of doing it.

If we were to do it using the alternative method, the code for that part would look like this:

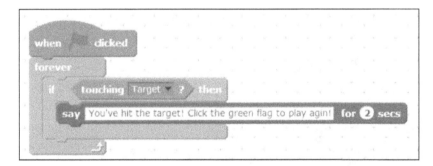

Using the timer

A timer can be a very helpful tool in a game. You may want the game to only last a limited amount of time, or you may just want to know how long the game has gone on for. In this recipe we'll explore this functionality.

Getting ready

There are two important blocks we'll use to work with timing in Scratch, both of which are under the **Sensing** category.

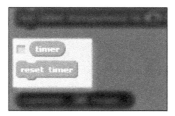

The first of these resets our time back to **0**. The second one allows us to place the time somewhere to be used, and also displays the time elapsed. Check the box next to the timer block so that we can see the time running on our stage.

> Notice that the time is kept in seconds, and does not count down. We'll figure out a few workarounds for this in *Chapter 5, Spicing up Games*.

We'll now have our game record the last time it took the user to hit the target. This will be stored as a new variable.

How to do it...

First, we'll need to create our variable that will handle storing the data.

To create the variable, perform the following steps:

1. In our set of code that places the mouse at its starting position, drag the reset timer block directly underneath the block. This will set the timer back to **0** each time we start the game over.

You may want to add the **reset timer** block below the other **placement reset** block in this set of code we created for the mouse. The way we have it set now, the timer will only reset when we start the game over ourselves, not when the mouse hits the wall.

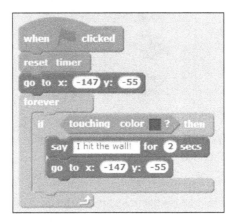

2. In the **Data** category, click on the Make a Variable button.

3. Name this variable `LastTime`. Be sure **for all sprites** is checked and click on **OK**.

In the sequence of code that is related to the target of the mouse, make the following adjustments to record the time:

1. Drag over a **change y by ()** block into the **forever** loop and set the value to **-20**. Place this above the **say () for () secs** block we had from before.

2. From the **Data** category, drag over the **set () to ()** block. Make sure the variable denoted is `LastTime`. Place this right underneath the last block we added.

3. Return to the **Sensing** category. Drag over the **timer** block into the **set () to ()** block value.

The final code of this particular script should be:

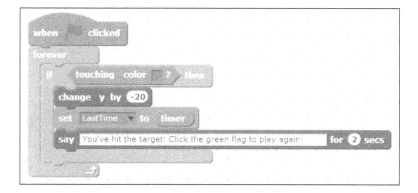

How it works...

What we've done here is move the value from the timer at the specific point in time where we hit the target to the value of the variable. The timer will keep counting, but now we have a record of what time we hit the target last.

Note that each time you hit the target, the variable will be changed. In our next chapter, we'll explore a way to keep track of multiple instances of time.

 You might be wondering why we added the **change y by ()** block here. This is because otherwise the mouse would continually be on top of the target, and thus meeting the condition we set. As a result, our LastTime variable would keep increasing and wouldn't be accurate.

See also

▶ The *Keyboard input into a program* recipe of *Chapter 3, Adding Animation*

5
Spicing up Games

In this chapter, we will cover:

- ▸ Tracking the best score or time
- ▸ Keeping a high score list
- ▸ Adding more levels

Introduction

This chapter will take us to the next level in creating games with Scratch. *Chapter 4, Basic Gaming*, focused heavily on learning some basic techniques in creating your first games in Scratch. Here, we'll extend this by exploring different ways to build upon what we've already done.

A lot of what we will deal with in this chapter requires working with variables, which we've used before for storing information, such as the score. We'll also learn a topic related to variables, known as lists. This helps us to store groupings of data.

We'll also take some time during this chapter to work a bit more heavily with the **Operators** category of blocks. These blocks perform various math operations for us, including addition, subtraction, multiplication, division, and much more. Here we'll work with a few of the basics, and learn more in *Chapter 8, Programming to Calculate*.

Tracking the best score or time

Often when we make a game where we are keeping track of score or time, it can be useful to know what the best score or time was. We can accomplish this goal rather simply using variables. Let's take a look at how to do this in this recipe.

Getting ready

This recipe will use the techniques we used in the last recipe named *Using the timer* in *Chapter 4, Basic Gaming*. Open up the Scratch file we had to create that recipe, we'll begin there.

 Recall that this was a game where we had a mouse crawl through a maze we created. We recorded the last time that it took to complete by using a variable. Here we will build on these ideas.

How to do it...

Follow these steps:

1. Head to the **Data** category of blocks. Click on the button to make a variable, as we've done in several recipes already.

2. Call this variable BestTime.

3. Take a look at the sequence of blocks shown in the following screenshot. This is what we'll be editing in this recipe:

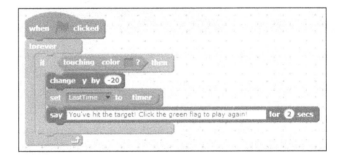

4. Drag a conditional block from the **Control** blocks category to the end of the **forever** loop as shown in the following screenshot:

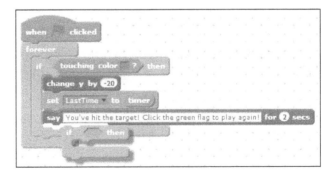

5. There are three logic blocks in the **Operators** category that are important here. Drag over and place it within the conditional block hexagon.

6. It is important to note that a logic block is one that performs a logical operation (such as the **() or ()**, **() and ()**, or **not ()** blocks. Under the **Operators** category of blocks you'll see three blocks that are used to compare numbers, they show symbols **<**, **=**, and **>**. Drag over the block and place it within the first of the hexagons shown in step 5.

> You might find it handy to check the checkbox next to all of your variables while you program. This will help you see what variables are for the purposes of debugging. You can then uncheck them later when you are finished.

7. Return to the **Data** category. Drag over the variable block **LastTime** into the first open spot from step 6, and then drag over **BestTime** into the second spot from step 5. It should look like the following screenshot:

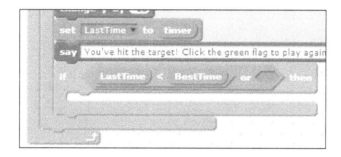

> This technique of placing blocks within other blocks is called **nesting**. We can nest blocks as much as we need to make our program perform as desired.

8. In our open hexagon shown in the preceding screenshot, drag over from the **Operators** category.

9. In the first open area, drag the **BestTime** variable block we used before.

10. In the second area, type the number 0. It should now look like the following screenshot:

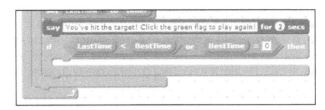

11. Now we'll focus on adding to what happens when the statement we just created is true.

12. Head to the **Data** category of blocks.

13. Drag the `set BestTime ▾ to 0` block. Be sure **BestTime** is the variable shown.

14. Replace the number **0** in the block in step 13 by dragging over the **LastTime** variable block in that place.

Your final script from what we started changing should be similar to the following screenshot:

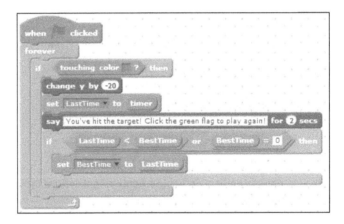

How it works...

You might be asking for a little insight into what we were doing here. Let's take a moment to break down the code from this recipe.

Recall that before we started this, the green flag was clicked on and a constant listener was created with the **forever/if** loop combination. Whenever the mouse is touching the color green (our marker on the maze) everything in the script would run. From there, the mouse would bounce downward by 20 pixels and **LastTime** would be set to the value of the timer at that moment. From there a congratulatory message appears telling the user to play again.

Next comes the new parts we just added. We started by bringing in a conditional statement. Everything in this conditional statement only runs when the condition we created is satisfied.

We essentially created a condition that will be true when one of two things happen:

1. The variable **LastTime** is less than the value of the variable **BestTime**. In other words, we completed the maze in less time in this round.

2. **BestTime** is equal to **0**.

The second part of the condition is necessary because the first time you run the program, the variable will be set to **0**. Obviously, your time will never be better than this. The condition ensures that your first run time will be recorded as the best time.

The last part is what is contained within our conditional statement as follows:

This part of the script is only completed if our condition is true, when a best time has been achieved. This block takes the variable **BestTime** and sets it to the value of **LastTime**. This is the part that actually records what our best time was.

This entire process is then repeated if the game is played over.

There's more...

We may wish to alert the player that they have beaten their previous score, or let them know if they did not. That is actually a pretty easy change to make, so let's give that a shot:

1. Pull the conditional block we had before outside of the current script and into the general workspace, as shown in the following screenshot:

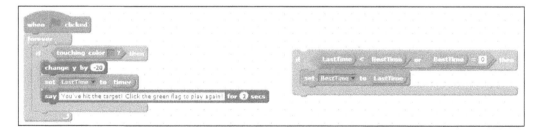

2. From the **Control** blocks category choose the **if-else** block as shown in the following screenshot:

3. Drag this block to where you removed the conditional block from.

4. Replace the hexagon in the new block with the contents from the condition in the old block.

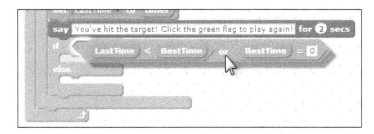

5. Next, place the contents of the conditional block into the first open space of the new block, shown in the following screenshot, you can also remove the old **if** block:

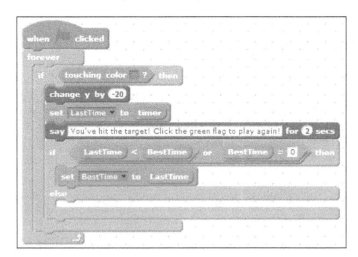

6. Open the **Looks** blocks category and drag over a **say () for () secs** block as we've used in many previous recipes. Place one of these underneath the block we just placed in the conditional statement area and also one in the **else** area.

7. Change the text of the first one to say `Congratulations, you've beaten your best time.`

8. Change the text of the other one to say `Sorry, that was not your best time.`

The final code you have should appear as follows (including previous code we have worked with):

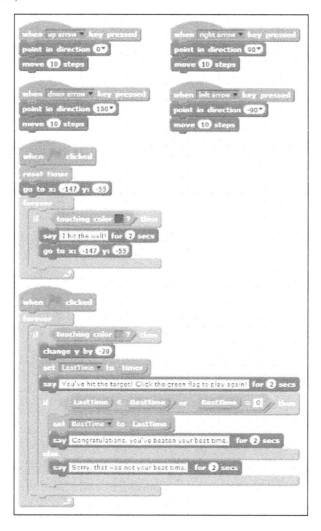

It is worth noting that the process we followed here is almost identical to what you would do if this were keeping track of a best score. You would simply need to change some of the variable names to match more appropriately, and you may want to use some different comparisons of previous scores in the conditional blocks.

Keeping a high score list

At times it may be beneficial to keep track of a list of several scores or times in a game. In this recipe we will learn how to do that. In particular, we are going to continue with the maze game we have been working on by adding a list of the top five scores. Note that we are not only creating a list of five items, but also sorting them to be sure we are presenting them in the correct order.

Getting ready

Begin by opening up the file we used for our maze game after completing the previous recipe *Tracking the best score or time*.

The main change we are going to be focusing on will again be in the same script as we previously changed, and will involve a new **variables** block that we have not come across yet.

Take a look at the **Data** set of blocks. At the bottom we see a button **Make a List**, marked in the following screenshot:

Using lists is much like dealing with variables, so the easiest way to practice is to jump into how we get this recipe going.

How to do it...

Follow these steps:

1. Click on the **Make a List** button demonstrated in the preceding screenshot.
2. Give your list a name. We'll call ours TopTimes. Click on **OK** once you have finished typing the name. Ensure **For all sprites** is selected before clicking on **OK**.

3. You'll notice several new blocks appear in the **Data** category. These are what we'll use to modify the contents of our list.

4. Drag the conditional statement we created in the previous recipe out of the script so it looks like the following screenshot:

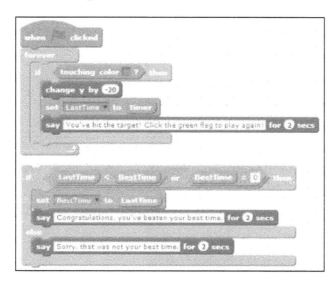

5. Remove everything from the second set of scripts in the image so you only have a basic **if-else** block:

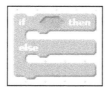

6. Drag the ⟨ ⟩ block into the conditional statement and change the right value to 6.

7. Under the **Data** category, drag a `length of TopTimes` block to the left open area of the block from step 6.

8. Create a new variable; call this variable `Index`.

9. Drag the **set () to ()** block into the **if** area of the conditional block. Change the variable to be `Index` and the value to be 1.

10. From the **Control** blocks, drag over a **repeat ()** loop `repeat 10`. This should go directly underneath the block from step 9. Drag over the `length of TopTimes` block into the value (replacing the number **10**).

11. We now need to drag in a regular conditional block into the **repeat** block. Your code so far should look like the following screenshot:

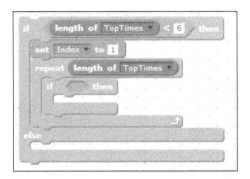

12. Return to the **Operators** area and drag over the 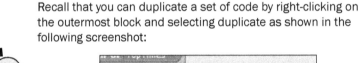 block into the conditional statement area.

13. Place a **() < ()** operator block in the first hexagon and an **() = ()** operator block in the second hexagon.

14. Drag in the variable **LastTime** into our first open spot.

15. Drag the new block  into the second open area. Replace the number **1** with the variable **Index**.

16. In our third open spot, place a duplicate of what you created in step 15.

 Recall that you can duplicate a set of code by right-clicking on the outermost block and selecting duplicate as shown in the following screenshot:

17. Leave the last open box blank. Your code as of now should look like the following screenshot:

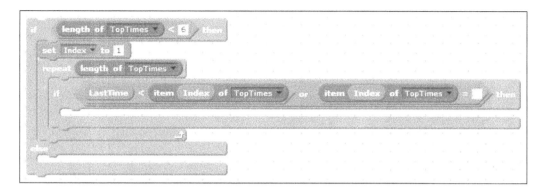

18. Drag over 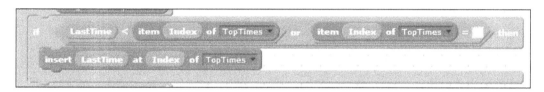 from the **Data** category. Place it in the **if** statement we have just created.

19. Drag over the variable **LastTime** into the first open spot replacing the word **thing,** and drag over the variable **Index** into the number spot. It should look like the following screenshot:

20. Drag over a **broadcast** block from the **Events** blocks and place it directly after the **insert** block.

21. Give the name `GameStopped` for the broadcast message to be sent.

22. Underneath the block from step 21, drag over a **stop ()** block, also from the **Control** blocks. Set this to **stop this script**.

23. Off to the side, drag over the top hat block labeled **when I receive ()** from **Events**.

24. Attach to this a **say () for () secs** block. Change the text to `Click the green flag to play again`.

25. Return to the set of code we were working with before. Beneath the **If** statement, drop a **change () by ()** block from **Data**. Set this to be the variable **Index** changed by 1. Your code so far should look like the following screenshot:

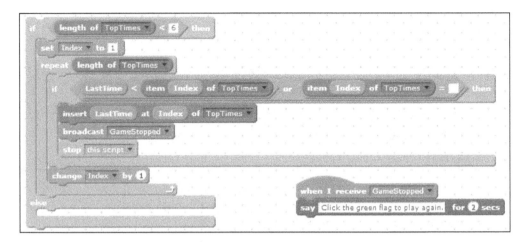

26. Now in the **else** area of the code, we need to add a few things. Drag a **set () to ()** block, with the variable **Index** indicated, and leave the assignment value as **0**.

27. Drag beneath this a **repeat ()** loop from the **Control** blocks.

28. In the space indicating how many times this loop should repeat, under the **Data** category drag the option for **length of TopTimes**. It should be coming together like the following screenshot:

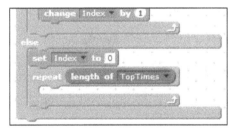

29. Place an **If** block within the **repeat** loop we just dragged in.

30. In the condition for the **If** block, begin by dragging 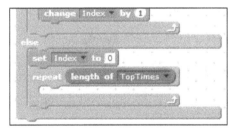.

31. In the left space, drop the variable **LastTime**. In the right space, drag in **item (1▼) of TopTimes ▼**. In place of the number **1**, drag over the variable **Index**.

32. Inside the **if** statement we have, drag over from the **Data** category the **insert () at ()
    of ()** block that we used. The last space should already have **TopTimes** in it. Drag the
    variable **LastTime** to the first space and the variable **Index** to the second space.

33. Beneath this drag a **delete () of ()** block. Change the numerical value to 6 from the
    default of **1**.

34. Similar to that, drag over a **broadcast ()** block as well as a **stop this script** block.
    Set the message to be GameStopped, the same as before.

35. Below the **if** block, drag a **change () by ()** block from **Data**. Change the variable
    to **Index**.

    The nearly-final code should be like the following screenshot:

36. Connect this new code with what we had previously in this recipe to obtain the following:

How it works...

For this recipe, we actually have quite a bit of code going on, so it's certainly worth examining. In fact, you'll probably want to go piece-by-piece through this code yourself at your own speed.

You'll notice we only changed the program past the **say** block in the main set of code, so we only need to look at that. The overarching block here is the **if-else** block we have. Recall that this block is useful in branching off in two possible directions. In one case, when the condition is true, a certain thing happens. In all other cases, the **else** part of the code runs.

We could actually nest several **if-else** statements to create multiple conditions with one catch-all condition at the end. Just continue to drag over more **if-else** statements into the **else** part of the upper level block.

One of the techniques we've talked about before is called nesting. You'll notice that we used this technique a lot here. Recall that nesting means we are essentially placing blocks within blocks to create the code we want. We actually nested all sorts of code with this sequence, including loops, operators, variables, and so on.

Within the first part of the **if-else** sequence, notice the condition we created:

This condition checks to be sure we have five or less times in our list of top times. We want to maintain a list of five, so if the list has five or less we'll need to add the new one. Or else, situation would deal with cases where we have more than five.

We used the less-than operator to compare two values here. In this case, we compared the length of **TopTimes** to the number **6**. This is a useful block that returns a number, specifically the number of items in whatever list it is set to.

Assuming the condition is met, we then created the **Index** variable. An **Index** variable is used to keep track of our location in a loop. Each time a loop is run, we increment this **Index** variable to let the program know where it is in the process.

 We always want to think about what our **Index** variable is set at when we use loops, and make sure we are resetting it before any looping process starts. If we assume the variable is set, it may in fact not be set. This could cause our program to run out of control.

After we've set our **Index** variable, we created a **repeat** loop. This loop is set to repeat based on the number of items in our list.

 A **repeat** loop in Scratch is also known in other programming languages as a **for** loop. We define at the start of the loop how many times we want it to run, and then the loop runs the code that is inside, just like following a repeated pattern. **For** loops are some of the most commonly used loops in programming.

We'll notice that next is a nested **If** statement. We created a somewhat complex condition to this one, so we'll want to really take a look at it:

We want the five best times to be listed in a specific order—from the best one to the worst one. We already know we need to add the time we're looking at to the list, since our first condition was true. Now we just need to find the place to put it on the list. To know if we have the right spot in the list, the variable **LastTime** either needs to be less than the list item in question, or there has to be no list item in that spot.

Notice we first used the **or** operator. As long as one of these conditions is true, the whole statement is true. On the left-hand side, we have our basic check to see if the variable in question is less than a specific item in our list of top times. We have to check each time the item where our index variable is at. This is a common practice. The **Index** variable will start at 1 each time, and then just increment. The second part simply checks to see if the list item has nothing in it.

Once the condition is verified, the value of our last time is placed in the spot of the **Index** variable, thereby adding it to the list. Next comes our **broadcast** command, which tells the program to say that the game has stopped, and then the script itself has stopped.

We might have wanted to not use the **broadcast** block here, since we could have simply put the **say** command in its place. This is so the code can keep going, and if we wanted more to continue unrelated to this we'd have a way to do so. You could also add the **insert** statement into the broadcast receiver to reduce duplication of code.

Now we have to take a look at the **else** portion of the block. This is the case where we already know that the list has enough items, we just need to check and see if the time we just completed is better than any of those current items in the list.

Our verification here is that the value of **LastTime** is less than the item in the list specifically numbered by the **Index** variable. If the value is less, then the script within the **if** statement runs. The value is placed (as shown previously) in the appropriate space in the list. We'd observe that the list would then be six items. To take care of this, we'd now delete the sixth item on the list. We then broadcast the same message as before to restart the game.

Notice that if the **if** statement is not true, the loop is repeated until it has gone through the entire list. We can also see that we need to stop the script in both of these cases so we don't go through the entire list and replace each item with the new value. We only want to change the one appropriate value.

There's more...

Here is an alternative bit of code that you might use to keep this recipe even simpler. That is one of the wonderful aspects of programming—that we can do the same thing in many different ways!

See also

For more information on nesting, see the previous recipe on *Tracking the best score or time*.

Adding more levels

This recipe is all about adding additional levels to your game. We're still going to work with the maze we've been working with in other recipes, so open up the Scratch file where we left off previously.

Note that you do not have to have finished the recipe on keeping a high score list to complete this recipe. In fact, you can do this recipe without having finished anything else in this chapter! Just keep in mind that a few things may look different in our pictures, and you still need the Using the timer recipe of *Chapter 4, Basic Gaming*.

Getting ready

One of the first things to note when adding new levels is that there will be a few different places where we just have to add minor pieces of code.

The first thing you should do is think about what you want your maze to look like. Before we get going, make sure the stage is selected. Just as we did with making our first background, paint yourself a new background. Note that you'll want to use the same wall color to keep your program working as it was before. Once finished, it should look something like the following screenshot:

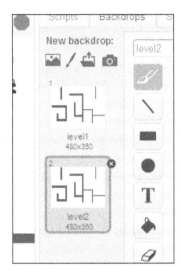

For simplicity in this game, when you click on the green target, the level changes. Now we're ready to get going!

How to do it...

1. Have the target (recall this is the green circle we used to end the game) as the selected sprite.

2. From the **Events** blocks, drag over a **when this sprite clicked** block.

3. Drag over a **broadcast ()** block under the block from step 2.

4. Create a new broadcast message, call it `levelChange`.

5. Now, select the stage. Note that the stage is a special type of sprite that displays backgrounds.

6. Drag over a **when I receive ()** block. Select the **levelChange** broadcast message to be received.

7. Drop a **next backdrop** block from the **Looks** category underneath.

8. Create a new variable called **Level**.

9. Drag a **set () to ()** block from the **Data** category. Make sure the variable selected is **Level**.

10. From the **Looks** category, find the block called **backdrop #** and drag it into the value for setting the value for **Level** from step 9. It should now look like the following screenshot:

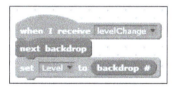

11. To make the game restart at level 1 when the green flag is clicked, drag over a green flag block and a **switch backdrop to ()** block to the stage script area. Also, attach a **set () to ()** block, setting the variable **Level** to 1.

12. Select the **Mouse1** sprite.

13. Drag over a **when I receive ()** block to create a new script.

14. Drag over a **wait () secs** block.

15. Drag two **If** statements directly below the block mentioned in step 14. You should have the following:

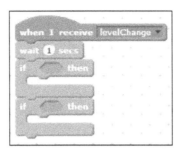

16. In the first condition, drag from the **Operators** category the ▭ block.

17. In the first open space, drag the variable **Level** from the **Data** category. Enter the number 1 in the second space.

18. Drag over the same block from step 15 to the next condition. Fill the first open space with **Level** again as we did in step 16. Enter the number 2 in the second space.

19. In the first **if** statement, duplicate the **go to x: () y: ()** block that we used to reposition the mouse after the game was reset.

20. Drag over another **go to x: () y: ()** block to the second block. Make the **x** and **y** values in this block the values for the location of the mouse when the game is set to the second level. Your code should look like the following screenshot:

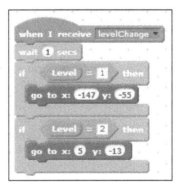

21. Recall that we had this set of blocks previously:

22. Duplicate the code we just created beyond the **if** statement (right-click on it and select duplicate as shown in the following screenshot):

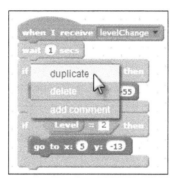

23. Drop the additional code in place of the third block shown in the code from step 20 we created in a previous recipe:

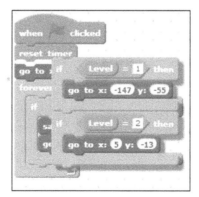

24. Remove the **go to x: () y: ()** block that was already in place. Replace the second one that was in the **forever** loop the same way. You should end up with the following result:

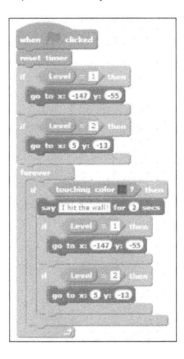

25. You should now be set to use the green target circle to change between levels. Test it out a bit.

Note that for **Mouse1** we have something similar to the following screenshot:

For the stage we have something similar to the following screenshot:

And for the target we have something similar to the following screenshot:

How it works...

There are a few new programming concepts that we used here, and we should take some time to explore them.

First we notice that everything starts when we click on the target. Essentially, by creating this small amount of code as shown in the following screenshot, all we set was a listener on the target.

This just means that the target waits to be clicked on, and when it is clicked on, it broadcasts a message to the rest of the program.

We had two other key places that reacted when the target was clicked, which are shown in the following screenshot:

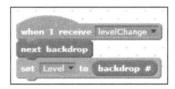

And then we also have something similar to the following screenshot:

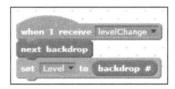

These two sets of code are starting simultaneously. The first operates on the stage and is what changes the background. The message is received and the background is changed. In order for other parts of the program to be able to detect what level we are working on, we set the variable **Level** to whatever background number we have selected.

In the second set of code, we added the **wait** block so we could ensure that the variable **Level** had been set to the correct level. This is necessary since we have simultaneous code running at once.

> We could have added in an additional **broadcast** and **receive** block as well instead of using the **wait** block. If we were running something that was potentially tedious on the stage, this might have been a better approach to take.

We then have two **if** statements to be concerned with. We've designed it so there is one **if** statement per level. When running through these, the game checks to see which level we are on and then resets the position of the mouse to the appropriate place. This is important so the mouse is always starting at the starting place for the level it is on.

We then edited the original code which placed the mouse at its starting place. This was so the game would not always reset to the level one position.

There's more...

We might wonder how we could accomplish the goal of incorporating additional levels. The idea is still the same, we simply add more **if** statements and more backgrounds. This principle also works similarly if we have a multiple level game. The convenience of using the broadcast-receive method is that we can start the process of changing multiple things on the screen with one simple broadcast.

Also note that we could have set the game to switch to the next level automatically when the mouse touched the target each time. To do this, we would simply require to add a **broadcast** block as shown in the following screenshot:

You also may wish to keep two separate lists of times for each level. This would only require that we create a second list and adjust our **if** statements. We could also use nested lists (this is too complicated to get into detail here; however, you could store lists within lists).

6
Bringing in Sound

In this chapter, wc will cover:

- ▶ Playing sounds
- ▶ Importing a new sound
- ▶ Recording a sound
- ▶ Playing drums and notes
- ▶ Adjusting volume
- ▶ Fading volume out
- ▶ Changing the tempo
- ▶ Interactive note playing

Introduction

You might have some interest in creating programs that have sound in them. This is the chapter where we will finally learn how to do that. Scratch has many built-in blocks that allow us to do this. Notice in the block palette there is an entire category dedicated to Sound.

Following is a screenshot of what you should see if you examine this category of blocks:

The recipes in this chapter will explore just a few ways that you can integrate these blocks. Some recipes will focus on just a short technique, while others will integrate a technique into a recipe you've seen before in other chapters. Sounds can be integrated in very basic ways, such as just adding a quick sound bite, or very complex ways by adjusting things such as notes played, tempo, and so on.

Let's get started with our first recipe!

Playing sounds

The most basic thing we can do with sounds in Scratch is simply playing a sound. Scratch makes it nice and easy to incorporate a variety of types of sounds into any program we create. This first recipe will involve making our default sprite make a meow sound when it is clicked on.

Getting ready

To begin, create a new Scratch file. We'll be using the default cat sprite, but you can change it if you'd like. While you can add sounds into any of the previous programs we've created, we're going to keep it simple by making the sound the entire focus of this program.

How to do it...

Let's get started with the following steps:

1. From the **Events** blocks, drag over the  block.

 If you change the name to the sprite, the block we just added will reflect that name change. As we've mentioned before, for more complicated programs, you'll want to make your sprite names more meaningful than the default names. This helps keep things organized.

2. Head over to the **Sound** category of blocks and drag over the **play sound ()** block.
3. Drop the block directly beneath the block we dragged over in step 1. The final code should look like the following screenshot:

4. Test this out by clicking on the cat; you should hear a **meow** sound with each click.

How it works...

The code for this recipe is rather simple. We have our top hat block that gets everything started. Recall that blocks like these are referred to in programming as listeners. This listener is activated when the sprite is clicked on with the mouse.

From there, the sound contained in the **play sound** block is played. In a more advanced program, this could include a variety of other blocks of code as well.

There's more...

You may find that you need to play a sound for an extended period of time and you don't want the longer sound to be interrupted by other code. If you use the code shown in the following screenshot instead, it will cause all of the attached blocks to wait until the sound is done playing:

See also

Check out the next recipe on *Importing a new sound* if you don't want to stick with the **meow** sound used in this recipe.

Importing a new sound

Scratch comes with a variety of sounds built-in that we can use beyond the default meow sound. Here we will see how to access them and get them into our programs to be played back at various points.

Getting ready

Refer to the previous recipe to have the ability to play a sound in your program. You may also apply this recipe to another program you have already added sound to using your knowledge from the previous recipe.

How to do it...

Let's get started:

1. You'll notice on the top of the script area there is a third tab we have not used yet called **Sounds**. Click on this tab. You'll see the following screenshot:

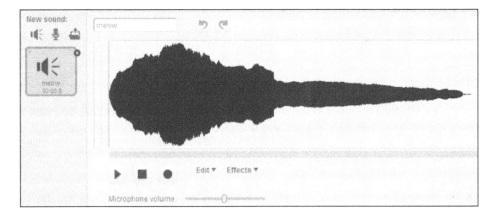

2. Click on the **Import** button that looks like a speaker. The following dialog box will appear:

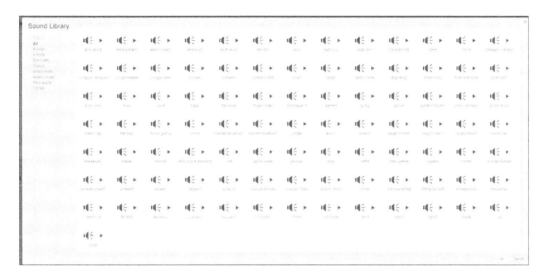

3. Choose a category of sounds from the list of categories, this will open up a variety of choices of sounds to use.

4. We'll import from the **Music Loops** category. Once you open a folder, you can click on the sound once to hear it previewed for you. We'll import **cave** into our program.

5. You'll now see the following in the sounds list:

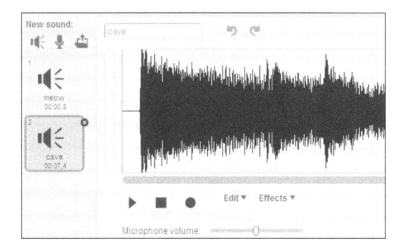

6. If you don't plan to use the **meow** sound anymore, you can delete it using the small circular **x** in the upper-right corner of the file size and name.

Just as you did with costumes and sprite names, you can adjust the sound names too so they will be more recognizable when you use them in your program.

7. Return to the **Scripts** tab.

8. Click on the drop-down arrow on the **play sound ()** block. You'll see your new sound as an option to play:

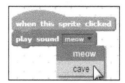

How it works...

This recipe is similar to the previous one; the only change is changing the background sounds available in our program. Similar to how we've imported multiple costumes before, we can import multiple sounds. This makes them available for our use in the program.

It is also worth noting that sounds are sprite-specific. When you import sounds into the program, you are making them available for that sprite only. You can also import sounds into the Stage, just as we did when selecting backgrounds.

There's more...

Scratch 2.0 includes a few new features when working with sounds. If we take a look back in the Sounds area, we see now we have various effects we can apply to our sounds:

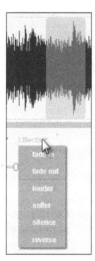

We can now highlight sections of the sound or apply effects to the entire clip of sound.

You might also be wondering how to go about uploading your favorite mp3 file to Scratch from your computer. You'll notice that in the same area we used to access the database of sounds Scratch has, we also have a button for importing from our computer:

You can use this button to navigate through files on your computer to find any song you like!

See also

See the previous recipe in this chapter on inserting a sound in general. Coming up next is *Recording a sound* to learn how to make your own sounds.

Recording a sound

Sometimes you may not be satisfied with the large variety of sounds that are already available in Scratch. That's OK, you can create your own! That's what this recipe focuses on.

Getting ready

This recipe follows from the previous two; however, you can also integrate this recipe into other programs you are creating.

Open a new Scratch file and program it to play a sound, see the previous two recipes if necessary.

 To record a sound, you will need a microphone on your computer. You may wish to buy a separate one, or you can use one built into a webcam you have.

How to do it...

Follow these steps to get a sound recording:

1. Go to the **Sounds** tab of the Script area, as we did to import sounds.

2. There is a button next to **Import** that says **Record** (shown in the following screenshot). Click on this button:

3. The Sound Recorder box (shown in the following screenshot) will then be visible:

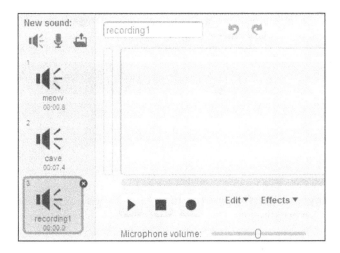

4. When you are ready to record, click on the record button (grey circle). You'll notice the sound bar change as the noise level changes. If it gets too loud for good quality, it will become red. You can see it at a reasonable level in the following screenshot. You'll also notice the timer increases as you record longer:

5. Once you've finished recording, click on the stop button (grey square) to stop recording.

6. Playback your sound recording by clicking on the play button (grey arrow).

7. If you are satisfied with the recording, you are done.

8. The sound will now be in your list of sounds, just as the rest. You may also wish to change the name, as was mentioned in the previous recipe.

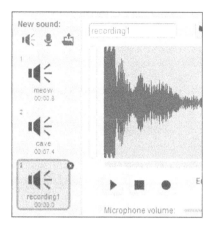

You can now access this sound through the same methods of playing a sound we've worked on previously.

See also

If you want to use your recorded sound in a script, it's done the same way as described in the first recipe of this chapter.

Playing drums and notes

This recipe will be dual-purposed for us. We will use this as a time to explore how to get help from Scratch for things you need a little extra guidance for, while also learning how to get Scratch to play drums and sounds.

Getting ready

Let's start by looking at the help area for blocks. Notice that in the area above the stage where the green flag is there is a question mark button. You can use this button to click on things you need help with in Scratch. Start by opening the help area for the first **drum** block:

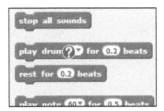

The tips panel will open on the right-hand side of the screen and you'll be able to navigate to the appropriate block. You'll see the following box appear with information on this block:

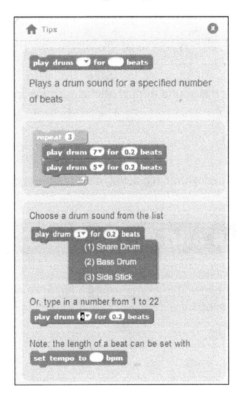

Not only do we get a bit of information on the block, we also get an example of how it can be used.

We'll now go into a variation on what they suggest. We'll create a beat that continues until you click on the red stop circle near the green flag on the stage.

Keep in mind that you can use the techniques in this recipe to create a large variety of sounds (even real music). The sounds created in this recipe are for illustration purposes, not to sound good.

How to do it...

Get this recipe going with these steps:

1. Drag over a `when    clicked` block from the **Events** blocks category.

2. Attach a **forever** loop below it from the **Control** blocks category.

3. Return to the **Sound** category and drop two **play drum () for () beats** blocks into the loop.

4. Drop a **rest for () beats** block beneath these.

5. In the first drum block, use the drop-down arrow to select a different **drum**, as shown in the following screenshot:

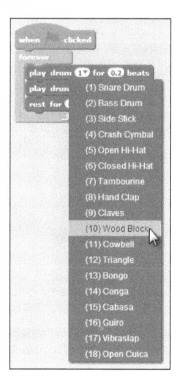

6. For the second drum, we selected drum **14**.

7. If you test this now, when you click on the green flag, you should hear two drum beats followed by a rest. The code you should have thus far should be as follows:

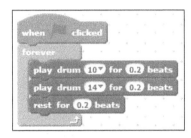

8. We'll now add a similar set of scripts to play notes on a keyboard.

9. Add a second sequence of blocks with a green flag top hat block and a **forever** loop as we did before.

10. Drag into this new **forever** loop two **play note () for () beats** blocks.

11. On the second block, click on the drop-down arrow, you should see the following:

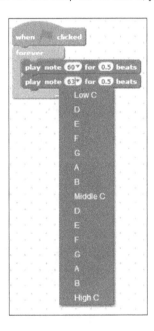

12. You can select the note to play by moving your mouse over the keyboard and clicking on the note you want. Notice we have typed in note **63**.

13. Now, you should have the following scripts all together. Test it out!

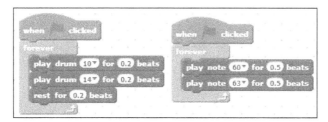

How it works...

You'll notice now when you play what we have in the preceding screenshot, it doesn't sound particularly good. In fact, you'll probably want to turn it off quickly! The point is though that you have parallel programming happening at once. Think of it as somewhat like an orchestra (or a band) playing. Everyone has their role to play with a specific instrument. If we mixed many of these we could have a great band!

There's more...

If you don't want to take the time to figure out how to create your own good tune, use the following code to play Twinkle, Twinkle Little Star. We've broken it up for you to make it easier to follow when putting it together (notice that there are only three different sets of code, so you can use duplication for the other three sets).

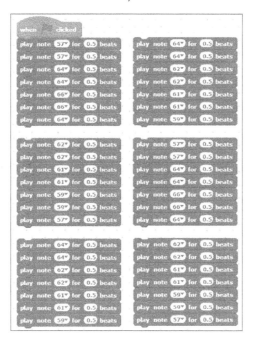

Place some rests between the code to set up your final tune!

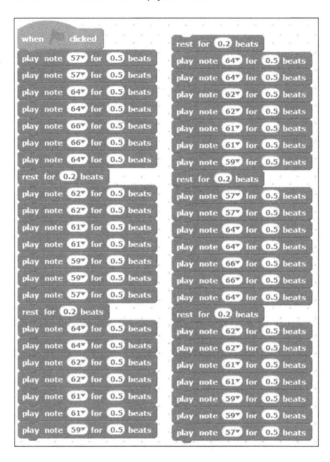

 In your final code, this should all be connected. It was just too long to show here in one set.

Adjusting volume

Sometimes we'll want to be able to change the volume of a sound in the running program using specific blocks. We're going to take the recipe we just finished and add two commands. One will increase volume, the other will decrease volume. We'll use the arrow keys on the keyboard to accomplish this.

Getting ready

Open up the last recipe we worked on. The only purpose of using the last recipe is that we have a variety of sounds to hear. We could actually use any other program with sound as well.

How to do it...

These steps will get this recipe set for us:

1. Be sure you are in the Script area for the sprite with sound. The volume we will change is specific to each sprite.

2. We need the volume reset each time the program starts, so drag in the `set volume to 100 %` block. It should be placed once under each top hat block we had before. It will in total look like the following screenshot:

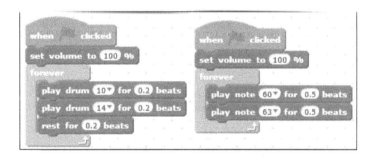

3. Under the **Events** blocks, drag over two `when space key pressed` blocks.

4. Change one to show **up arrow** and the other to say **down arrow**.

5. Return to the **Sound** category.

6. Drag the **change volume by ()** block beneath each of the new top hat blocks you just placed.

7. Change the one for the **up arrow** to be a positive 10. You should have built the following:

8. Now start the program. Press the up and down arrows at various points to test. You should hear the volume change accordingly.

See also

Take a look at the next recipe to see how to use this technique to fade sounds out completely.

Fading volume out

Sometimes it is desirable to make a sound fade out. We'll continue by building code similar to other recipes in this chapter and then fading the sound out.

> You could do this with notes, drums, or just general sounds. It all still applies just the same!

Getting ready

Open a new file and create the following code. If you need a reference, see the first few recipes of this chapter:

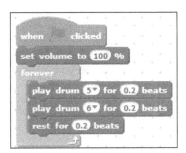

How to do it...

To get working on creating a volume fade, follow these steps:

1. Drag over a new block.

2. Attach a **wait () secs** block from the **Control** category and change the time to 20.

3. Drop a **forever** loop below this.

4. Return to the **Sound** category. Drop a **change volume by ()** block into the **forever** loop you just created.

5. Change the numerical value to -5.

6. Return to the **Control** category and drop a **wait () secs** block below the **Sound** block you just dragged in.

7. Change the wait time to 0.5 seconds.

8. You should have the following code that will play for 20 seconds and then begin to fade out.

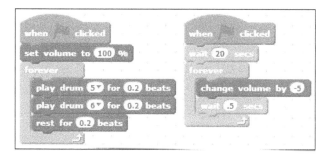

See also

You may also want to take a look at the recipe on *Playing drums and notes* or the recipe on *Adjusting volume*, both of which are earlier in this chapter.

Changing the tempo

The last set of blocks we have in the **Sound** category can help us adjust the tempo of the notes we play. That just means how quickly or slowly the beats play.

 The default tempo in Scratch is 60 beats per minute. The default value of the **change tempo by ()** block is 20. This is good to keep in mind if you begin to change the tempo a lot.

What we'll do now is take a familiar block of code and change the tempo by clicking on the sprite.

Getting ready

Take this block of code from a previous recipe and create it in a new file:

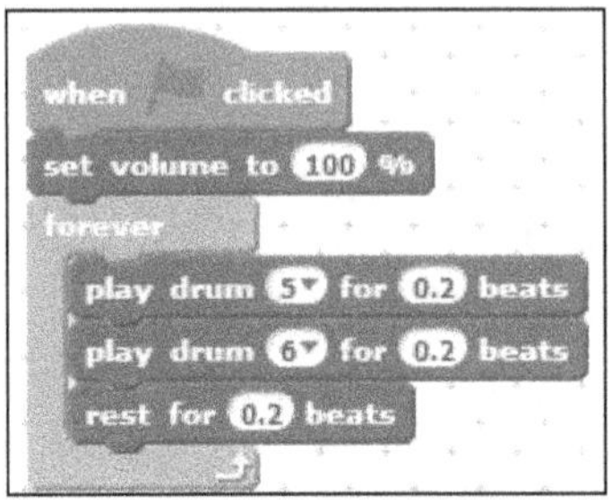

You'll notice in the **Sound** category the following three new blocks:

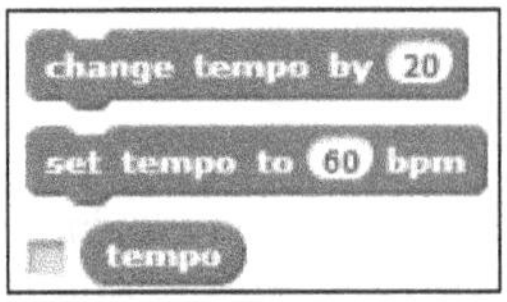

We'll now take a look at these.

How to do it...

To change the tempo in your program, follow these steps:

1. Drag the **set tempo to () bpm** block between the green flag top hat block and the volume setting block, as shown in the following screenshot:

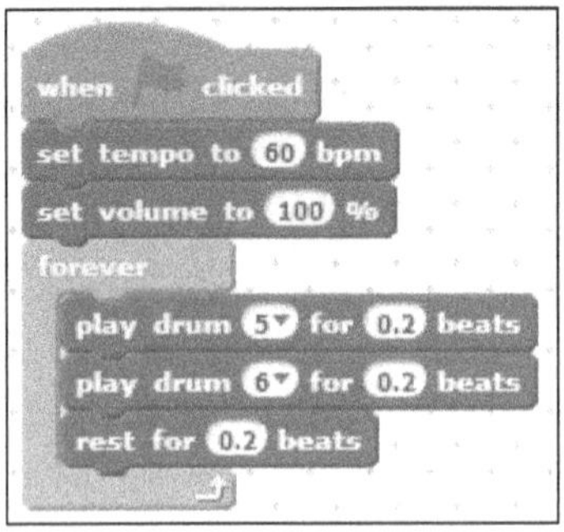

2. From the **Control** blocks category, drag the  block to create a new sequence.

3. Place a **change tempo by ()** block below this, as shown in the following screenshot:

4. Now test your program. As you click on the sprite, the speed the drums are beating will increase. When you click on the green flag again, they will go back to normal.

Interactive note playing

In this recipe we are going to create a program that integrates many techniques we've used already in this book with the use of sounds. Specifically, we are going to create a program that asks the user for three notes to play and an instrument number. The program will then take the user input to play a tune.

Getting ready

Not much is required to get this recipe moving. First, open up a new Scratch file to use. You can customize the appearance through either picking a background or a new sprite if you'd like, though this is not necessary. Here we will work strictly with the default sprite and white background.

How to do it...

Follow these steps to get this recipe set:

1. Create four new variables; name them `First note`, `Second note`, `Third note`, and `Instrument`.

2. Drag over a new `when clicked` block and place it in the Script area.

3. Below the top hat block you just dragged over, select the **say () for () secs** block from the **Looks** category.

4. Replace the text in the block from step 3 to say `I am going to play 3 notes you select`.

5. Under the **Sensing** category, drag over the **ask () and wait** block to be the third block in the sequence. Change the text to `What is the first note you'd like to play (number 0-127)?`

6. From the **Variables** category, drop in a **set () to ()** block. Set the variable to **First note**. In the second open area, drag an **answer** block from **Sensing**. Your code until now will look like the following screenshot:

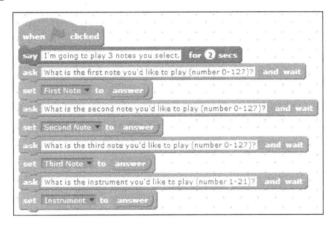

7. Replicate the last two blocks of code three more times including the variables **Second note**, **Third note**, and **Instrument**. The text of the last **say** block should be changed to **What instrument should I play (number 1-21)?** It will then look like the following screenshot:

8. Drag a **say () for () secs** block into the script. Add the text `Great. Now I will play a tune with those notes.`

9. From the **Sound** category, drag over the ![set instrument to 1] block. Within this block, drag over the block for the variable **Instrument**, as shown in the following screenshot:

10. At the end of the sequence, drag over a **forever** loop from the **Control** blocks.

11. Drop three 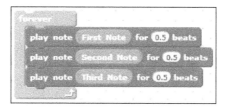 blocks within the **forever** loop.

12. Replace the note number with the first, second, and third note variables, as shown in the following screenshot:

13. Your final code will then be as follows:

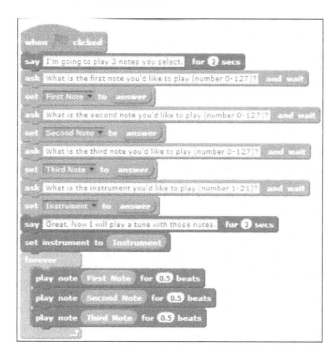

14. Test out your program, you should hear the notes you've chosen. Play continuously until you use the red stop button to end the script.

How it works...

Most of the blocks we work with here are ones we've used before. One technique we do a lot here is nesting.

Note the cases where we dropped a variable into another block where otherwise we would either type a number or select one from a list. We also did this with the answers to the questions our program is asking the user. This strategy is important, and useful, because it allows us to set settings through user input and allows variation in the program. Take for example the last instances of this within our **forever** loop. The logic we used for this is to make the program continuously (that is, forever) play the first note, then second, followed by the third. Each time the block goes to play a note, it checks to use the number stored in the variable.

Note that we have two lists we are dealing with in this recipe. The notes, which go from the number 0 through 127, as well as the instruments, which go from number 1 through 21.

As a reference, you can use the drop-down arrow to see more about these notes, or you can use the help setting we talked about earlier in this chapter.

7
Integrating PicoBoards

In this chapter, we will cover:

- ▶ Setting up the sensor board
- ▶ Getting values from the sensor board
- ▶ Working with the slider
- ▶ Integrating the light sensor
- ▶ Integrating the sound sensor
- ▶ Measuring resistance
- ▶ The sensor board button
- ▶ Checking other connections

Introduction

Up until this point, all we have used for user interaction in our programs is the keyboard and mouse. In this chapter, we will talk about using a sensor board to interact with Scratch. Specifically, we are going to discuss using the brand referred to as PicoBoards, by PicoCricket (`http://www.picocricket.com/`). The specific PicoBoard we're using in this chapter can be purchased from `https://www.sparkfun.com/products/10311`. At the time of writing the cost was $44.95 plus shipping. A mini USB cable is not included, so you'll want to purchase one of those from any cable supplier. Note that there are other types of sensor boards (and even other outside devices) that can be integrated with Scratch. In fact, some have set up the Microsoft Kinect, Nintendo Wii, Arduino, and more. The PicoBoard is used here as an example of some of what you can do. You should always feel free to explore other technologies!

It is also worth noting that this chapter is the only chapter in this book that is based on the older version of Scratch, Scratch 1.4. This is because at the time of publication the Scratch creators haven't finished adapting the PicoBoard functionality to Scratch 2.0. This is expected to be available later in 2013. You can download the older version of Scratch from `http://scratch.mit.edu/scratch_1.4/`. You'll notice that much of the recipes built for Scratch 2.0 in this book will also work with version 1.4.

PicoBoards have several different sensors that allow you to get input from the outside world and have your program interpret the information. The following image shows the PicoBoard we use and the various sensors that are on it:

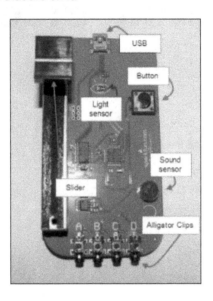

We can see that the largest sensor shown is the slider, which takes up the entire length of the board. We can also see a small dot outlined by an eye directly below the USB connection port; this dot is the light sensor. Near the light sensor opposite to the slider is a button we can use. Next to the button is the sound sensor. Lastly, we see four connections labeled **A**, **B**, **C**, and **D**. These are the four resistance clips (also known as alligator clips) that come with the board.

Most of the recipes in this chapter will focus on basic techniques of things you can do with the sensor board. The last recipe will combine many techniques you've already learned in previous chapters with a few that we'll learn in this chapter. By the end of this chapter, you'll be ready to create plenty of programs using the sensor boards. So let's get started!

Setting up the sensor board

Let's work through this recipe to get our sensor board set up.

Getting ready

The first step is physically setting up the PicoBoard, getting your computer set up to recognize it, and then setting up Scratch to know it is there. These are all things we are going to take care of in this recipe so that you are ready for the rest of the chapter to dive into using the sensor board.

How to do it...

Follow along these steps to get your PicoBoard ready to go. Do not connect the PicoBoard to the computer until you are instructed to do so in the following steps:

1. Download the most up-to-date drivers for your board from http://picocricket.com/whichpicoboard.html.

2. You'll be asked to determine if the board has a serial connection or USB. If you purchased your board from the link mentioned in the preceding step, it is most likely a USB connection. You can identify a USB connection as a slim, rectangular shaped plug on the computer end. A similar, but smaller, version of that plug will plug into the board.

3. You'll see at the top of the page that you are directed to three options for drivers: Windows XP, Windows Vista/Windows 7, or Mac OS X. Download the appropriate file for your computer.

 While the directions will be similar for all three operating systems, we are using Windows 7 here, so there may be slight variations in the upcoming instructions. While a version for the drivers is available for Linux, support is not offered for Linux by the manufacturer.

Open the `.zip` folder that you just downloaded. Run the application and approve any messages that are given to you (similar to the one shown in the following screenshot). You will then see a command prompt briefly pop up as the driver is installed. Note that you may see different messages depending on your operating system settings:

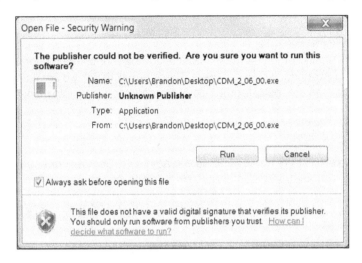

4. The next step is to connect the PicoBoard to the computer. First connect the small end of the USB cable to the board, as shown in the following image:

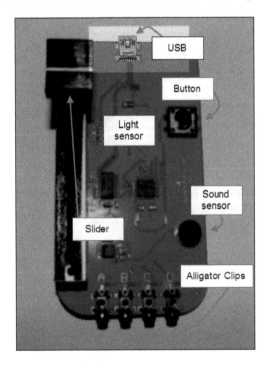

5. Now connect the other end of the USB cable to your computer, shown here:

6. We are almost ready to begin creating projects using the sensor board in Scratch. Open Scratch to begin configuring Scratch to receive data from the board.

7. Examine the **Sensing** category of blocks. At the bottom of the list you will see the following two blocks we have not used yet. In the *How it Works...* section of this recipe, we'll talk a bit about why these two blocks are different.

8. You should enable remote sensor connections by right-clicking on either of the two blocks shown in the following screenshot, and selecting the option **enable remote sensor connections**:

9. Windows 7 will probably show a firewall allow window. You should click on **OK**.

10. To be sure the sensor board is ready to go, we need to make sure Scratch is receiving data from the board. Right-click on either of the two blocks shown in step 7.

11. Click on **show ScratchBoard watcher**.

You will see the following information block pop up on the stage. This shows us all of the data that Scratch is receiving from the sensor board:

12. Play around with the sensors (for example, push the button, slide the slider, and so on) on your sensor board. If no numbers change on the list shown on the stage, continue with step 11. If values do appear, you are ready to go!

13. Right-click on the list and choose **select serial/USB port**.

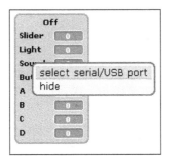

14. A list of ports will appear going through all options from 1 to 32. Begin to select working your way down the list until you begin to receive data from the sensor board.

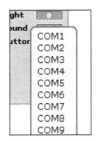

15. Once you see values in the watcher, Scratch is ready to go.

16. An optional step: right-click on the watcher and choose **hide** to make it disappear again.

How it works...

The primary concept we need to understand in the procedure for setting up Scratch to operate with your sensor board lies in the communication between the hardware and software. When going through the steps, you would have probably noticed that to get info from the sensor board we use the following two blocks:

As we have drop-down menus in each, you may be wondering why both are not built into one block. The answer is because there are two types of data that are returned from the sensor block.

The first type of data is a value, or in other words, a number. This number is then stored in this temporary variable (the block) until you use it somewhere (such as storing it in a variable you created for this purpose), or it changes on the sensor board. The slider, light sensor, sound sensor, and the four resistance sensors (alligator clips) all operate this way and use this first type, returned with the first block shown in the preceding screenshot.

We also have data that is stored as `true` or `false`, based on the result of some sort of statement (we call this a conditional statement because it depends on a condition). This second type of data is what we call a Boolean data type. For example, what we see in the second block shown in the preceding screenshot is the **button pressed** Boolean. If the button is pressed, the sensor board will return to the computer that the button is pressed (`true`). If the button is not pressed, it will be returned as `false`. This type of block may be inserted somewhere we need to verify something, such as our conditional loops that attach conditions (like the button being pressed) to our code. Aside from the button, we also have a way to see if the alligator clips A, B, C, and D are connected.

See also

 ▶ You may want to visit `www.picocricket.com/picoboard.html` for additional information on getting yourself going with the PicoBoard

Getting values from the sensor board

This recipe will get us ready to do all of the fun things a PicoBoard can do. We'll start off with the basics of getting some data from the sensor board.

Getting ready

Open up a new Scratch file to use. This recipe will strictly focus on storing the data from a sensor as a variable, so will be relatively short in length.

How to do it...

Follow the steps:

1. Create a new variable called **Slider Value**.

2. Drag over a [when ⚑ clicked] block (remember, this is in the **Control** category in Scratch 1.4, but in the **Events** category in version 2.0).

3. Drop a [set Slider Value to 0] block underneath the block from step 2. Note that in the older version of Scratch this is in the **Variables** category, but this category was renamed **Data** in version 2.0.

4. Now we will use one of our new blocks from **Sensing**. Drop the  block as shown in the following screenshot:

5. You should now have the code shown in the following screenshot in your script area. You can now use the variable as you would for any other variable in Scratch:

How it works...

This is a similar idea to some of the other things we've done previously in this book. We're taking what is a temporary variable that can change at any moment, that is, the sensor value from the following:

And, we are storing it as a more permanent variable.

 Are you struggling to understand the difference between storing the value from a temporary variable in a standard variable and from a permanent variable in a standard variable? Think of it as a set of cups. One cup is being poured into the other. In the case of this recipe, the cup we are pouring is the sensor value from the slider, and we are pouring into the permanent variable. Keep in mind though, permanent variables can be changed—we do that a lot. What we mean by a permanent variable is that it is a variable created for a specific purpose.

We can also compare this process to using ask What's your name? and wait and answer blocks. The first block compares to the process of getting data from the slider. Our second one compares to the actual temporary data we attain with our block. In essence, these work the same way. The only difference is that the answer block can be any string of characters, not just a number.

There's more...

Here are a few additional pieces of code you could use the slider value for; we'll go in depth even more in the next recipe.

All of these start with the variable setting we did in this recipe, followed by:

Verifying the value:

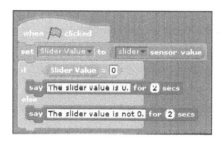

We can check a value and make a statement, similar to other recipes we've done before.

Setting a color:

As a nice, simple approach, you can use the slider to set the graphic effects.

These are just a couple of options! We'll see in the next recipe the concept of adding in loops to do continuous things with the slider.

See also

▶ Check out the *Working with the slider* recipe to go more in depth with the slider

Working with the slider

We've seen from the previous recipe that the slider can play a valuable role in working with basic programs. The slider can be very useful anytime you need a number in a range, and want that to be sensitive for the user to control.

In this recipe, we're going to dig deeper into using the slider. We are going to make a basic program where our sprite will move up and down as the slider moves.

Getting ready

We'll accomplish this by having a **forever** loop that is constantly checking the slider value, and applying it.

Open a new Scratch project to get started on this one.

How to do it...

Here are the steps we will need to get this recipe going:

1. Drag over a 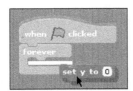 block.
2. Insert a **forever** loop directly below this top hat block.
3. From the **Motion** category, drag a **set y to ()** block, as shown in the following screenshot:

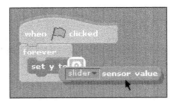

4. Head over to the **Sensing** category and drag a **() sensor value** block, replacing the value of 0 from the block created in step 3.

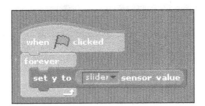

5. You should now have the following code, and if you click on the green flag, as you move your slider the sprite should move accordingly:

There's more...

An alternative way to use the slider could be to build in some rotation function to your program. The following steps would accomplish this:

1. Drag a 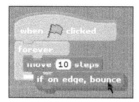 block to the script area.
2. Drop a **forever** loop below the top hat block you just added.
3. Within the loop, place a **move ()** steps block from the **Motion** category.
4. Drag over an **if on edge, bounce** block from the **Motion** category.

5. Under the block you dragged over in step 4, drag a **wait () secs** block from the **Control** category. You should now have the following:

6. In the sprite settings area above the script area, set the second setting that will restrict your sprite from rotating all around. Refer to the *The Hello World project* recipe of *Chapter 1, Getting Started with Scratch* if you don't recall how to work with these settings.

We now have what we need for the sprite to move around the screen. The part we'll add now will change the angle the sprite is moving at with the slider.

1. Drag over another  block to create another sequence of code within the script area.

2. Insert a **forever** loop directly below this top hat block.

3. From the **Motion** category, drag a **turn () degrees** block:

4. In the **Operators** category, drop a **() - ()** block within the block from step 9, as shown here:

5. In the first open set, drag a **() sensor value** block. In the second open set, type in the number 50. You'll then have the following:

6. If you run your program, you should now be able to see the sprite move across the stage and rotate constantly as you change the slider.

> Why did we subtract 50 from the value of the slider? The slider values only go between 0 and 100. If we want to rotate in a different direction, we need to have negative numbers. This makes it so we've moved the range of values to -50 up through 50.

See also

▶ Refer to the *Integrating the light sensor* recipe that will deal with the light sensor of the PicoBoard

Integrating the light sensor

The light sensor, pictured in the following figure, can detect changes in the amount of light nearby. We can use the sensor for doing things such as detecting shadows or increase in light.

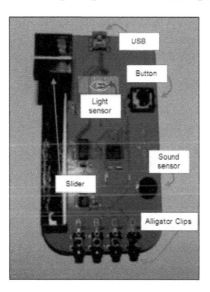

Getting ready

In this recipe, we are going to explore working with values from the light sensor. We will make a simple program where the sprite brightness will correspond to the amount of light coming into the light sensor.

Keep in mind as we go through this recipe, the light sensor returns values similar to the slider. Values will range from 0 to 100, 0 representing no light.

How to do it...

Let's get started with some steps that will get us there.

1. Open up a new Scratch file. As always, you can customize the sprite or background to match your preferences.

2. Drag over a **when ⚑ clicked** block.

3. Insert a **forever** loop directly below this top hat block.

4. Drag over the  block from the Looks category, and you'll have:

5. Change the effect selected to be **brightness** by clicking on the drop-down arrow in the block:

6. Now drag a **() sensor value** block into the value for the brightness effect.

7. Similar to what you did in step 5, change the sensor to the **light** sensor in the block from step 6, as shown here:

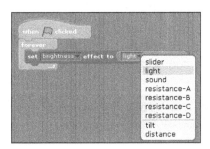

8. Now we are ready to test the code by clicking on the green flag. After clicking on the green flag, move your hand over the sensor slowly and see if it works! You should see the brightness change as you move your hand over the sensor. Your final code appears as follows:

Note that here we are using the strategy of taking data directly from the sensor without using a variable, unlike what we did earlier.

See also

▸ Check out the *Integrating the sound sensor* recipe, a similar type of sensor to the light one

Integrating the sound sensor

The sound sensor can be a useful tool in getting your program to interact with the outside environment.

Just like the other blocks we've used so far, the sound returns a value between 0 and 100. It is simply a measure of how loud the area around the sensor is, and it is not a microphone.

Getting ready

In this recipe we are going to explore the sound sensor by making the cat make a meow sound when a loud noise is detected by the sensor. To prepare for this, all you need to do is open a new Scratch file.

How to do it...

Here are the steps we'll need to get this going:

1. Drag over a [when ⚑ clicked] block.
2. Similar to the **forever** loop we've used before, we can also use the **forever if** loop. Drag it into the sequence.

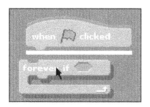

3. Under the **Operators** category, drag over a **() > ()** block into the conditional spot of the **forever if** loop. (Note that in Scratch 2.0 this loop doesn't exist, and we build it using the **forever** loop and **If** statement.) You should have this code now:

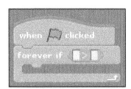

4. Within the first open spot, drag a **() sensor value** block from the **Sensing** category.

5. Use the drop-down arrow to select the sound sensor.

6. Type the number 75 into the second open spot.

7. Go to the **Sound** category and drag a **play sound ()** block within the loop.

 You'll have the meow sound selected automatically if you are using the default sprite. If you want to use another sound, or are using a different sprite, head to *Chapter 6, Bringing in Sound* to learn about changing the sounds.

Your code should now be:

8. Lastly, drag the **wait () secs** block from the **Control** group beneath the **play sound ()** block. The final code will be:

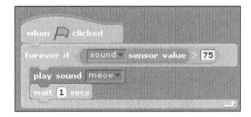

How it works...

There are a couple of notes that are good to make in this recipe on how things are working. First of all, we are using a loop we have not used much before this. The **forever if** loop is essentially a combination of two loops:

This basically accomplishes the same as:

This block can be very useful anytime you need to attach a condition to a loop. In this recipe, we are creating a listener that will wait for the condition to be true. Once the listener determines the statement is true, everything within the loop will run, which in the case of this recipe is simply playing the sound.

A second important operational note to make is why we used the **wait () secs** block. If you test out your program without this block, and make a continual loud noise, you'll notice that the meow sound will continually interrupt itself. If we go into the sound info, shown in the following screenshot, you'll notice the length of time the sound takes to play is one second. You could also use the **play sound () until done** block from the **Sound** category.

By adding this wait time into the block, enough time will be allotted for the sound to finish playing before it plays again.

 If you decide to use a different sound, make sure the time the program is waiting to repeat corresponds to the amount of time that sound takes to play.

A last note to make is why we used the number 75. Our loop, as we set it up, defines a loud sound as one that is 75. This is only a preference, and in your own program you may choose to set it higher or lower.

There's more...

If you don't actually have a PicoBoard, but want to integrate sensing from sound into your program, you have an alternative!

In the **Sensing** category, you'll see the following two blocks:

Both of these blocks detect the level of sound from any microphone you have connected to your computer. The first of these, the **loudness** block, detects the level of noise from 0 to 100, just as the sensing block does. The second of these, the **loud?** block, stores Boolean data and returns either true or false on whether or not the environment is loud. On a scale from 0 to 100, loud is 30 and above.

See also

▸   Refer to *Chapter 6*, *Bringing in Sound*, where sound is discussed more in detail

Measuring resistance

Resistance, which can be thought of as how easily electricity flows through something, can be measured (informally) using Scratch. This recipe is going to get us going in collecting resistance values.

Getting ready

This will be a recipe that will work with the resistance of two different items, so we'll use two sets of alligator clips. We'll create a program that will check the resistance of two objects, and will let the operator know which object has a higher resistance.

Set up the PicoBoard with two of the alligator clips, as shown here:

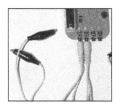

Now you're ready to get started!

How to do it...

Follow these steps to make our program that will check the resistance of two objects:

1. Open a new Scratch file.

2. Drag over a block.

3. Drag three **if** statements underneath the block from step 2. This will result in the following:

4. Drag one of each of the three blocks from the **Operators** category that compare values into the conditional statements you just created.

This should result in the following:

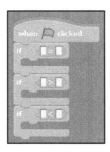

5. In the first open block of all three of these, place a **() sensor value** block from the **Sensing** category and set these to **resistance-A**.

6. In the second open block of all three of these, place a **() sensor value** block from the **Sensing** category and set these to **resistance-B**. You'll then have the following:

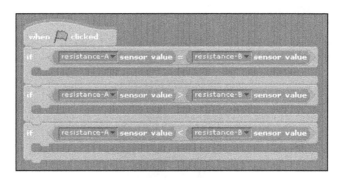

7. Create three **say () for () secs** blocks from the **Looks** category as shown in the following screenshot, with the same text:

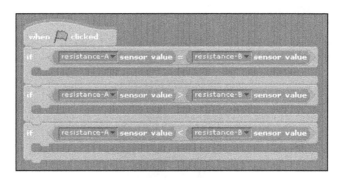

8. Drag the blocks you created in step 7 to the appropriate conditional statements you have. This should then give you the final code:

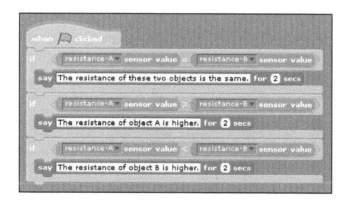

9. Test out your code by connecting various things to your alligator clips (some options include paper clips, pieces of wire, paper, or aluminium foil). The following is an example of testing a paper clip with foil:

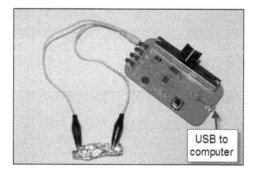

USB to computer

How it works...

The main concept to understand about this recipe is how these three conditional statements operate. We created three different **if** statements that cover all possibilities for resistance. Once the green flag is clicked, each condition will be checked and will only be true if statements will run.

There's more...

We can expand on this recipe in two related ways.

First, let's have the program tell the user when the sensor measures zero resistance for both the objects. Here is how we do it:

1. Follow steps 1-8 outlined in the *How to do it...* section of this recipe to get the following code:

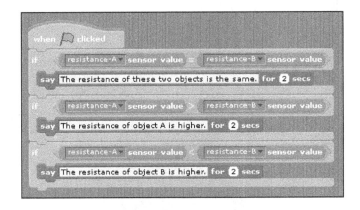

2. Insert an **if** block within the first **if** statement, as shown here:

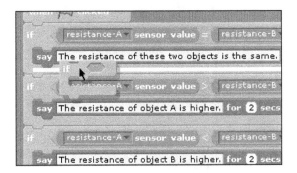

3. Drag over the **Operator** block containing the equals sign into the **if** condition.

4. In the first open block of the operator, place a **() sensor value** block from the **Sensing** category and set this to **resistance-A**.

 Notice that we only check the resistance for A. This is because we are nesting this code within the code that already checked the resistance of both and found them to be equal. We could have just as easily checked the resistance for B to be 0 instead.

5. In the second block, type the number `0`.

6. Now from the **Looks** category, drag a **say () for () secs** block into the **if** statement you just created.

7. Set the text for the block to be `The resistance for both objects is 0.` You'll now have the following:

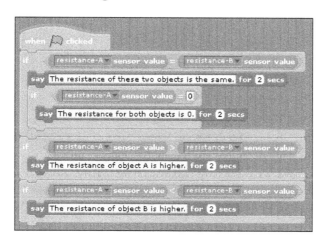

Another extension of this recipe would be to have our program tell the user what the specific values are for resistance. Add the following steps to do this:

1. Make a variable and call it **Text**:

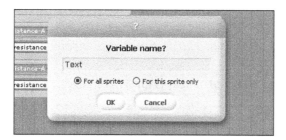

2. We need to use this variable to store the text we want to display. Drag the **set () to ()** block to somewhere in the script area.

 Sometimes coding like this that can get complicated, so it is helpful to create the code outside the original sequence and add it last.

3. Under the **Operators** category, drag  to within the variable declaration block from step 2.

4. We need to use this block to place two pieces of text together. Drag over an additional **join () ()** block into each of the open spaces from step 3, replacing **hello** and **world**. This will give you the following:

5. Replace the text of the first **hello** text by typing `The resistance of A is` . Note that you should have an extra space after you finish typing.

6. Replace the text of the second **hello** text by typing `and the resistance of B is` . Leave the same extra space on this one, as well as a space before the word `and`. You will have the following:

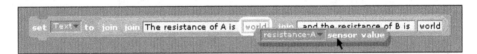

7. Drag from the **Sensing** category the **() sensor value** block and set it to **resistance-A**.

8. Repeat step 7 for the resistance of B.

9. Drag a **say () for () secs** block to the script area underneath the code you've been creating.

10. Drag the variable **Text** into the **say () for () secs** block:

11. Drag the entire set of code and place it at the end of the original sequence:

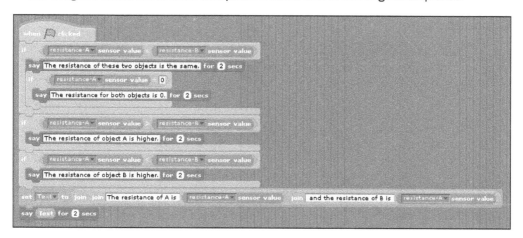

12. Now give your program a test run and make sure it works as expected.

The sensor board button

Our PicoBoard also has a built-in button, as shown in the following image. This can be handy for anything where you might want a button to be pressed in your programs.

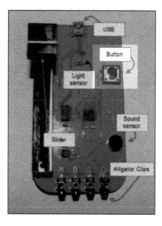

Getting ready

This recipe will explore checking to see if the button has been pressed. We'll do this by creating a program where the sprite will move across the screen when the button is pressed.

All you need to do to get this recipe ready is to open a new Scratch file and make sure your PicoBoard is fully functional. Also note that we are using a different sprite in this program called **duck1**:

Of course, you can use any sprite you'd like.

How to do it...

Follow these steps to implement button use in your program.

1. Drag over a `when clicked` block.

2. Drag in a **forever if** block from the **Control** category.

3. Drag from the **Sensing** category the `sensor button pressed ?` block into the conditional block from step 2. You'll have:

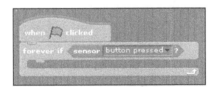

4. Within the conditional block, drag a **move () steps** block from the **Motion** category.

5. Attach to the block from step 4 an **if on edge, bounce** block, also from the **Motion** category.

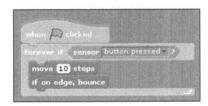

6. Adjust the sprite settings so that the sprite will only face left and right:

7. Now click on the green flag and try pressing the button on your sensor board. You should start to see your sprite move back and forth on the stage.

Checking other connections

Similar to how we checked to see when the button is pressed, we can also see when the alligator clips are connected (either directly together or with something completing the circuit between them).

Getting ready

This recipe will simply show you the technique for checking a connection between the clips.

Before following the steps in the next section, open a new Scratch file.

How to do it...

Follow these steps to get going:

1. Drag over a ▓▓▓▓ block.
2. Attach an **if** block from the **Control** groups below this.

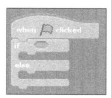

3. From the **Sensing** category, drag a **sensor ()?** block to the condition space. Set it to **A connected** using the drop-down menu.

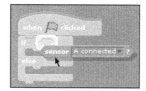

4. Drag two **say () for () secs** blocks to the script area and change the text as shown here:

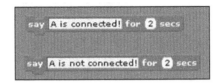

5. Drag the two blocks from step 4 into the corresponding area shown here:

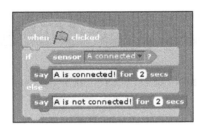

6. Now run your program, testing at least once for having the clips connected and at least once not having them connected.

There's more...

You might be wondering right now how useful this recipe is. To make it useful, we can expand on it and use the alligator clips to check when something else is connected. For instance, perhaps you want to create a race controlled by the players of the race; connect their alligator clips, which start the movement of their players.

8
Programming to Calculate

In this chapter, we will cover:

- ▸ Generating Fibonacci numbers
- ▸ Sieve of Eratosthenes
- ▸ Creating a password generator
- ▸ Other Scratch calculations

Introduction

This chapter focuses on using Scratch to do some calculations. One of the greatest uses of computers is to do tedious calculations to save time. This is because computers are very good at following a set of directions many times over—as we've seen through all the programming we've done so far.

We're going to work through three difference recipes in this chapter, two of which will do a lot of calculations for us very quickly. The third recipe will focus on creating a program that can be used as a basic password generator. Lastly, we'll play around with a few other ways we can make calculations in Scratch.

All of these recipes will focus heavily on the use of blocks we've used before, in addition to many new ones from the **Operators** category:

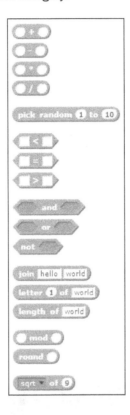

The blocks from this category allow us to do a lot of different mathematical computations on the numbers (usually stored as variables) in our programs.

Let's get going with our first recipe!

Generating Fibonacci numbers

You might be asking yourself what Fibonacci numbers are. What we're talking about is a sequence of numbers generated recursively (that means through repeated computations). Each new Fibonacci number is computed by summing the previous two numbers. The set begins with 0 and 1, and then builds from there.

If we compute the first few ourselves, we'd have:

Third number = First number + Second number = 0 + 1 = 1

This leads to the sequence 0, 1, 1, 2, 3, 5, 8, 13, 21, ...

Getting ready

We can see that generating these Fibonacci numbers can be a tedious task, particularly if we wanted to generate a lot of them. Luckily, we can use Scratch to generate as many Fibonacci numbers as we want.

Here, we will create a program that will do that for us (generating a maximum of 1,000 Fibonacci numbers). The output of these numbers will be a list of all Fibonacci numbers generated.

How to do it...

Follow these steps to work through this recipe:

1. Open a new Scratch file.
2. Create a new variable, call it **Generate up to**. Make the variable apply to all sprites.
3. Create a new list, call the list **Fibonacci Numbers**.
4. We'll also need an index variable later on; so create another variable and call it **Index**.
5. Deselect the checkbox next to the variable **Index** you just created so that it doesn't appear on the stage. Your **Data** category should now look like this:

6. Be sure the default sprite is the sprite you are programming for.

 Note that it really doesn't matter what sprite you use, we just need some place to store our programs.

7. Drag a block to the script area.

8. From the **Data** category, drag a **delete () of ()** block underneath. Change the first space to **all**. As we only have one list, the correct list is there by default. You should have the following:

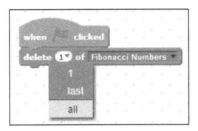

 So why are we deleting items from a list that has nothing in it? The answer to this is simple. There may be items in that list. After the first time we run this program, something will be there, as well as every time after. This guarantees that nothing is in that list to start with.

9. Drag a **set () to ()** block to the sequence. Declare that variable as **Index**. Change the value of the block to 2.

 We use the number 2 because we are going to deal with the third number in our list and work with numbers 1 and 2.

10. Drag over two **add () to ()** blocks, also from the **Data** category. Set the first one to 0 and the second one to 1. You should then have:

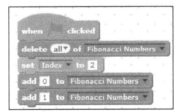

11. Drag a **repeat** loop to the script area from the **Control** category.

12. Place the variable **Generate Up To** into the value for the **repeat** loop.

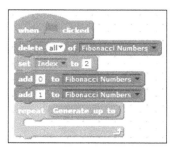

13. Now we'll create a separate (more complicated) piece of code that will later on be dragged into the loop we just set up. Start by dragging into the script area an **add () of ()** block.

14. Head over to the **Operators** category and drag an addition block into the value:

15. In the first space, drag **item () of ()** in from the **Data** category. Replace the value indicating the item with the variable **Index**.

16. Drag over another **item () of ()** block into the second open space.

17. Instead of placing the variable **Index** into the value of the list item, drag a subtraction operator in.

18. Place the variable **Index** into the first space of the subtraction operator and type the number 1 into the second space.

19. Drag over a **change () by ()** block to the block you've been building. Be sure the variable selected is **Index**, and the value should stay at the default number, **1**.

 This might be a good time to double-click a few times on what we are creating. You'll start to see numbers added to your list.

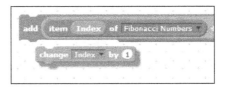

20. Drag this sequence of nested blocks into the loop from before. You should have the following:

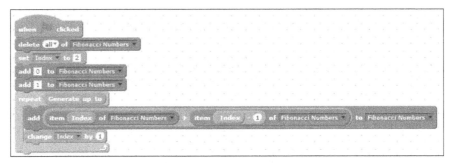

21. Now turn your attention to the stage, it probably looks like this:

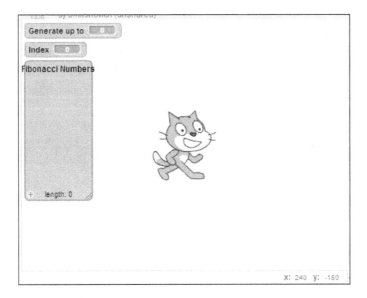

22. Right-click on the variable shown in the left-hand corner to get the menu shown in the following screenshot. Select **slider**.

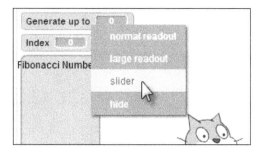

23. The variable should then be displayed as a slider. Change the value to some other number, as shown here:

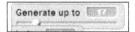

24. Deselect the **Index** variable by unchecking the checkbox back in the **Data** category.

25. Test out your program. You should see a list of Fibonacci numbers generated that looks something like this:

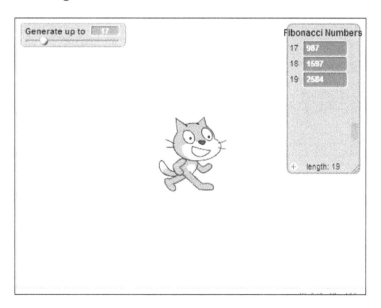

26. Note that you may also want to expand the size of the list by dragging in the lower right-hand corner. This would help you see more numbers at a time without scrolling:

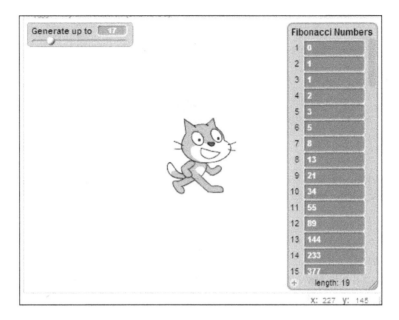

How it works...

This recipe has a lot going on worth taking a look at. Much of the logic used is similar to things we've done in recipes explained earlier in the book, so let's take a look at a few new pieces of code.

First of all, why did we add the numbers 0 and 1 to the list when we did this?

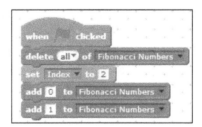

The answer to this question is we have to know that the list of Fibonacci numbers begins with the numbers 0 and 1. From these two numbers, each other number is built by taking the previous two numbers and adding them together. As our list starts off empty, we need to put the first two numbers in there to get things started.

We also might wonder what the purpose of using the **repeat** loop and **Index** variable was. We had to use the **repeat** loop to tell our program how many Fibonacci numbers we were looking to generate (based off of the variable set by the user—**Generate up to**. The **repeat** loop is set to run the number of times that variable is set to. Each time the loop runs, a new number is added to our list.

Now to break down the piece of code that actually adds the number to the list:

In this code we have quite a bit of nesting going on. The code actually adding the item to the list is the surrounding block we started with. This tells the program to add the number to the list.

The number shown is created by adding the previous two list items together (by the use of the operator). The use of the **Index** variable tells Scratch which two numbers are the previous two.

See also

▸ You might be interested in learning more about Fibonacci numbers. If so, you can check out http://mathworld.wolfram.com/FibonacciNumber.html

Sieve of Eratosthenes

This recipe is all about generating prime numbers. It is a known algorithm that can generate these numbers for us. An algorithm is a specific procedure (or set of instructions) that leads us to a result. If you'd like detailed information about how the algorithm works, you should take a moment to visit http://mathworld.wolfram.com/SieveofEratosthenes.html.

In a nutshell, the sieve works by determining if a number is prime by doing the following. You write down all of the numbers from 2 until your end point (let's say that we want to find all of the primes until the number 100 ; you'd write every number from 2 to 100). Next, go through each number from smallest to greatest and cross it out if it is divisible by 2. Then look at the smallest number in the list (in our case, 3). Beginning with the next number higher than 3, cross out each number divisible by 3. Continue this process until you've gotten to $2 + \sqrt{n}$, where _n_ is the number you were going up to. All of the numbers that remain will then be prime.

Getting ready

Start off this recipe by setting up a new Scratch file with the following.

Create the following variables in the **Data** category:

- ▶ **Current Prime Index**
- ▶ **End number**
- ▶ **Index**
- ▶ **Square root**
- ▶ **n**

Also create a list called **Numbers**. Select and deselect the variables as shown here to only show one variable on the stage and your list of numbers:

You are now ready to get going!

How to do it...

Let's work through the following steps in order to get our program going and generate some prime numbers:

1. Drag a  block to the script area.

2. From the **Data** category, drag a **delete () of ()** block underneath. Change the first space to **all**. As we only have one list, the correct list is there by default. You should have the following:

3. From the **Data** category, drag the **add () to ()** block. Make the value of the first space 2.

4. Drag three **set () to ()** blocks to the sequence of code. Set them up as shown here:

5. In the block related to **Square root**, drag an addition operator block to the value place holder and set the first number to 2.

6. We have a new block from the **Operators** category to drag into the open space we have:

7. Into the operator from step 6, drag the variable **End Number** so that you have the following:

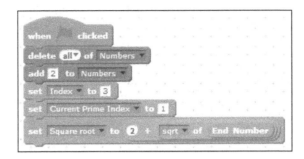

8. Drag a **repeat** loop to the script area with the **End Number** variable placed into the value for the loop.

9. Within the loop, drag the **add () to ()** block from the **Data** category.

10. Drag the variable **Index** into the first space of the block from step 9.

11. Inside the loop place **change () by ()**. Set the variable in this block to be **Index**. You should now have:

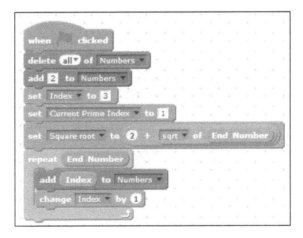

 Don't forget, as with variables, you can click on the checkbox to view the list for testing purposes.

12. Drag a new **repeat** block to the end of the sequence. Place the variable **Square root** into the loop condition.

13. Drag **set () to ()** into the loop. Set this block to be the variable **n** with a value of 1.

14. Beneath this block from step 13 drag yet another **repeat** loop. Set the condition in this one to the block `length of Numbers` from the **Data** category.

15. At the end of the loop you just created, drag a **set () to ()** block. Make the variable **Current Prime Index** and the value 1. You should then have:

16. Now in the loop that has nothing in yet, drag **set () to ()**. Make the variable indicated **Index**.

17. Place in the value for the block from step 16 an **item () of ()** block. Drag the variable **n** to the first open spot.

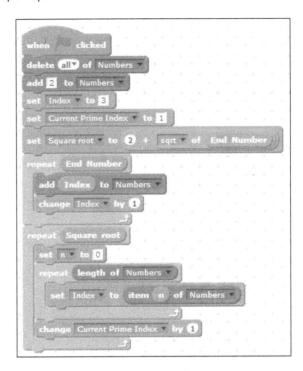

18. Within the most recently added repeat block, drag an **if** statement followed by a **change () by ()** block. Set the variable to **n**.

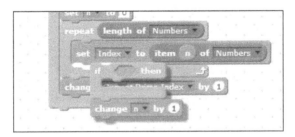

19. Next, drag a **delete () of ()** block from the **Data** category into the open if statement.

20. Drag the variable **n** into the first space of the block from step 19. You should now have:

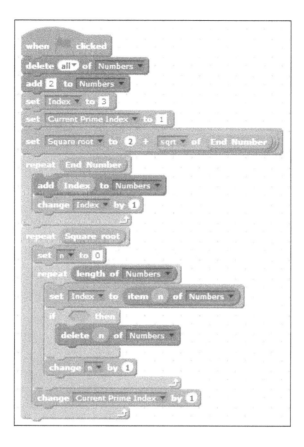

21. Now to set the condition of the if statement. We will build this off to the side, and drag it in last.

22. Drag over from the **Operators** category a **() and ()** block.

23. In the first space, drag over an equivalence operator to have:

24. In the second space, drag over a **not ()** operator.

25. We now have three open spaces. In the first space, place a **() mod ()** block, from the **Operators** category.

 The **() mod ()** block performs division for us and returns the remainder. For example, if we divide 2 into 5 (or 5 mod 2), the result is 2 with a remainder of 1, so the block will return 1. This is known as **modulo arithmetic**.

26. In the second space (still in the modulo block), type the number 0. You'll have the following:

27. In the first space for the **mod** block, place the variable **Index**. In the second space, drag **item () of ()**. Drag the variable **Current Prime Index** into this space so that you have the following:

28. In our last open space, drag an equivalency operator.

29. In the first new space created, drop the variable **Index**.

30. In the second space, drag **item () of ()**. Drag the variable **Current Prime Index** into this space so you have the following:

31. This large condition now needs to be dragged into the condition of our **if** statement, like so:

This makes our final code:

32. To set the stage, right-click on the variable and select **slider**. Change the value of the slider for testing.

33. Also expand the list shown on the stage so that you see more numbers without scrolling. Your stage should now look like this after running the program:

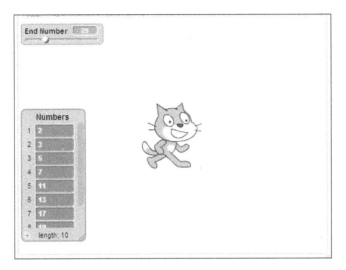

How it works...

Let's examine this recipe part-by-part:

This is the code that gets the most of our program set to run. It kicks things off with the green flag first, sets the beginning list parameters, and then declares several of our variables. Notice that we first delete all entries in the list to make sure none are left over, then adds the first list value, 2.

We use the variable **Index** as an index variable for several of our loops to let us know where we are in the loop.

We also use the variable **Current Prime Index** to indicate which prime number we are checking the divisibility of (first 2, then 3, then 5, and so on).

Lastly, we use the variable **Square root** to determine where we need to stop checking.

Our next sequence of code to examine is:

This part of the code is what controls adding all of the general numbers to the list to be checked in the next step. For instance, if our end number is 100, the program will go through and add the next 100 numbers after 2 to the list.

Lastly the following, is our most important part of code that carries out the actual algorithm we are working with:

This set of code has two **repeat** loops and an **if** statement controlling everything. We start with the outermost **repeat** loop, which runs the number of times necessary to ensure we've found all primes (recall what this is based on from the *Getting ready* section of this recipe).

We then set a new index variable, *n*, to 1. This will govern the next **repeat** loop that follows. We measure the size of the list, and then set that **repeat** loop to run that number of times. For example, if there are 100 numbers in the list, the loop will run 100 times.

The program then starts working through the list to see which numbers satisfy the condition:

If that condition is met, the number is deleted from the list. This condition is actually checking to see if the number from the list in question is divisible by the smallest number in our list. It is making sure that the number is not equal to the divisible number (thus eliminating 2 on the first round, 3 on the next, 5 on the next, and so on).

The first part of the condition involves modular arithmetic. When a number is evenly divisible by another number, there is no remainder. Modular arithmetic is checking for that here by asking if the index value is divided by the **Current Prime Index** value, is the remainder 0? If so, it is evenly divisible and the statement becomes true.

Once the statement is true, the number is then deleted from the list, as it cannot be prime.

This process is then continued throughout the entire list, resulting in a list that only contains prime numbers.

See also

▶   This project is loosely based/remixed on a project that can be found at `http://scratch.mit.edu/projects/AlanProjects/578654`. You may be interested in checking out that project as well, and reading the next chapter on remixing.

Creating a password generator

Creating passwords that are secure can be a bit of a challenge. Some of the best passwords can be generated by a computer. We'll create a program in this recipe that will generate passwords for us.

It is important to note that while it is beyond the scope of this book, the passwords we are creating here with this generator are not of the greatest strength. You can, however, use this as a baseline to create stronger passwords that would be much more challenging to crack.

Getting ready

To get started, open up a new Scratch file. Delete the default sprite and import a button from the `Things` folder.

How to do it...

Follow these steps to create our password generator:

1.   Increase the size of the button sprite you just imported to take up a decent amount of space.

2. Under the **Costumes** menu for the sprite, click on **Edit** and add the text **Generate** to the button.

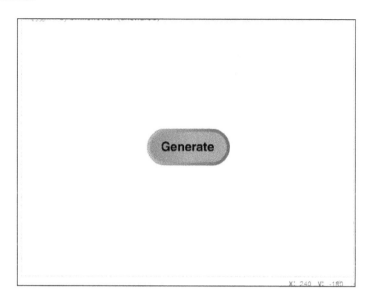

3. Drag a [when clicked] block to the script area.

4. Create a variable called **Password** and another called **Type**.

5. Create a list called **Characters**.

6. Under the block from step 4, drag a **delete () of ()** block from the **Data** category. Set the first open space to **all**, and leave the second at its default of the list you just created.

7. Drag 8 **add () to ()** blocks to the sequence and type in one character of each shown in the following screenshot. Remember that you can use duplicating to make this easier!

8. Connect the sequence of blocks from step 8 to the rest so that you have:

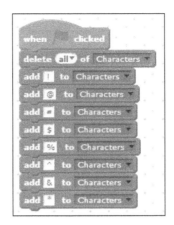

9. Create a new sequence of blocks by dragging over the top hat block **when this sprite clicked**.

10. Drag the **set () to ()** block next and make the variable **Type**.

11. In the value portion of the block from step 11, from the **Operators** category drag a pick **random () to ()** block. Set those values to 1 and 3.

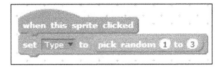

12. Drag over three **if** statements from the **Control** category.

13. Place an equal operator in each condition of the statements from 13. In the first space of each place the variable **Type**. In the second space, type 1 in the first, 2 in the second, and 3 in the third. You should have the following:

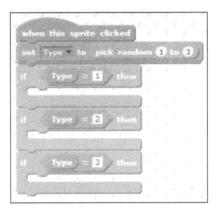

14. Within the first loop, drag a **set () to ()** block, change the variable indicated to **Password**.

15. Drag a **join () ()** block from the **Operators** category as shown in the following screenshot:

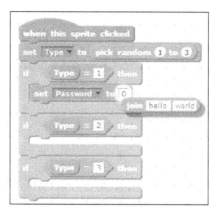

16. Repeat steps 15 and 16 for the next two **if** statements you've created so that you have the following:

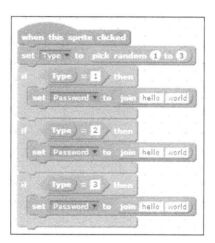

17. Return to the first containing block; in the first space of the joining operator place an **item () of ()** block from the **Data** category.

18. In the value space of the block from step 18, drag a pick **random () to ()** block. Set the range to 1 to 8.

19. Replace the word world with a **pick random () to ()** block. Set this range to 111111 to 999999.

20. In the second **if** statement, replace the words **hello** and **world** with the reverse of the first statement so that you have the following:

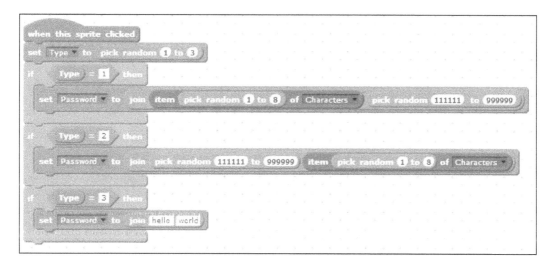

21. Now to build the last statement, place a second **join () ()** block within the one you already have there.

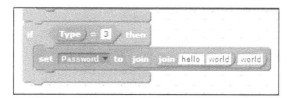

22. Replace the word `hello` with the block **pick random () to ()**. Make the values `111` and `999`.

23. In the first **world** spot, drag the same set of code (shown in the following screenshot) you've been using to pick a list item:

24. In the last **world** spot, duplicate what you did in step 23. You should now have a final sequence of code, as follows

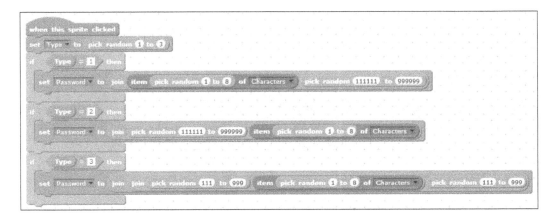

25. Turn your attention to the stage and right-click on the display showing the variable **Password**. Click on **large readout**.

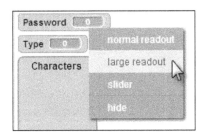

26. Right-click on the display for the variable **Type** and select **hide**.

27. Repeat step 26 for the list of characters on the stage.

28. Click on the green flag to be sure that your list has characters in it.

29. Click on the **Generate** button on the stage to begin generating passwords:

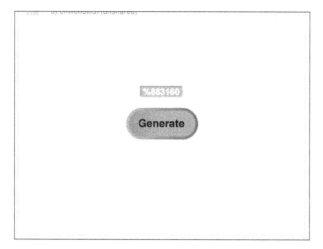

How it works...

As computers don't truly generate random numbers (they actually generate what are called **pseudorandom** numbers), we added a bit of extra "randomness" to this project. For instance, we wanted to build passwords that are more secure, so we added one character to each password from the list. We might have made this more secure by adding letters to this list, or by adding multiple characters. We selected a random placement of that character as well (either the first spot, middle of the password, or the last spot).

For further exploration, you might want to create more conditions on where the character is placed so it could end up anywhere in the password. You might also vary the length of the numbers that are generated (notice that we only used 6 numbers and one character).

Other Scratch calculations

Scratch (just like many other programming languages) has the capability to do some pretty advanced calculations. Here we will mention a bit more on the block that really helps us do a lot.

Getting ready

The block we are dealing with in this short recipe is the `sqrt ▾ of 9` block from the Operators category.

How to do it...

These are the two simple steps we need:

1. All you need to do is drag this block to any spot you would normally drag a number or variable (this block represents a temporary variable—one that is calculated on the fly).

2. Change the function you wish to perform from **sqrt** (representing the square root function) to whatever you want.

These functions are all interesting in their own regard, so we encourage you to do some research on your own to learn more about what all of these great mathematical functions can do. The opportunities are endless!

9
Project Remixing

In this chapter, we will cover the following recipes:

- ▸ Importing parts of other projects
- ▸ Drawing with the pen
- ▸ Remixing the pen project

Introduction

Creating your own projects is a lot of fun in Scratch. However, a lot of other people have had some great ideas for projects too! This chapter is all about taking something someone else has created and customizing it—we'll call that remixing. One important advantage of remixing projects made by others is to be able to also share what we do with others—that is the entire point of remixing!

We're going to go through a few recipes in this chapter that will remix work we've seen before. We'll begin with a simple recipe about learning how to import code from one project to another. Then, we'll create something new using some blocks we haven't come across yet. Next, we'll remix that project to do something else.

After this chapter, you'll be remixing projects (that you download) in no time! If you want to find out more about downloading projects, check out *Appendix, Collaboration*.

Importing parts of other projects

You may download a project from the Scratch website and just want to take parts of it for your own projects. This recipe is going to teach you how to do that. We'll see how to take a project and import it into something we've already been working on.

In Scratch 1.4, you were able to import an entire project into another Scratch project. With Scratch 2.0, it gets a little more complicated. What we'll do is take individual sprites and save them to our computer. We can then upload them back to Scratch (and use them in other projects).

Getting ready

Get started by creating something of your own. It doesn't make too much of a difference what you create, just have something there so you can see what happens when we import.

For our illustration purposes, we've imported the following sprite and background to our stage:

What we're going to do is export the dinosaur to our computer, which can then be used to import (along with the corresponding code) to our project.

How to do it...

Work through the following steps for this recipe:

1. Right-click on the sprite you wish to export.

2. Select **save to local file**.

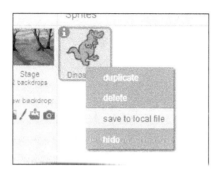

3. Navigate through the files on your computer and find a place to save the file.

4. Click on **OK**.

5. Your sprite (and the code that went along with it) is now saved to your computer. You can create another project and import that sprite to access/import that code.

6. Open a new Scratch file (or one you've used before) to test importing. Note that you could even test this out with the file we just created. For our example, we opened up the file from the *Keyboard input to a program* recipe in *Chapter 3, Adding Animation*.

7. Click on the **Upload sprite from file** button:

8. Navigate to the file you saved in step 4.

9. Your sprite, as well as the script that went with it, will now be in your other program:

Drawing with the pen

Pens are a category of blocks we can use to draw on the stage. This recipe will explore using the pen to draw a square on the stage.

This is a new category we haven't used before in the block palette:

Getting ready

All you need to do to get this recipe started is open a new Scratch file. We'll be using the default sprite. It may also be fun to add the grid background to the stage.

How to do it...

Follow these steps to draw a square on the stage:

1. Drag a green-flag block in to the script area.

2. Drag a **clear** block from the **Pen** category.
3. From the **Motion** category, drag a **go to x: () y: ()** block. Set both values to 0.

4. Drag a **point in direction ()** block in to the sequence. Change the value to 0. You'll now have the following:

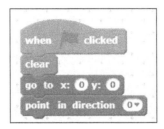

5. Drag a **move () steps** block. Change the value to 100.

6. Drag a **point in direction ()** block and change the value to 90.

7. Next, place a **set pen color to ()** block from the **Pen** blocks. Click on the color to select a color you like.

8. Drag a **set pen size to ()** block from the same category. Set the value to 3.

> If you'd like a thicker colored line, increase the value you set in step 8.

9. Drag a **pen down** block in to the script. You'll now have:

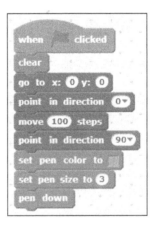

10. Drag a **move () steps** block and set the value to 100.

11. Drag a **point in direction ()** block. Make the value 180.

12. Drag a **move () steps** block and set the value to 200.

13. Drag a **point in direction ()** block. Make the value -90.

14. Drag a **move () steps** block and set the value to 200.

15. Drag a **point in direction ()** block. Make the value 0.

16. Drag a **move () steps** block and set the value to 200.

17. Drag a **point in direction ()** block. Make the value 90.

18. Place a **move () steps** block at the end with a value of 100.

19. From the **Pen** category, end the script with a **pen up** block. You'll now have the following:

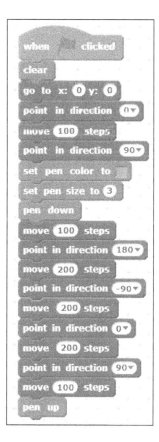

Now, if you click on the green flag, you'll see the sprite move very quickly in a square direction, and a square outline will be left on the stage.

See also

▶   In the next recipe, *Remixing the pen project*, we'll remix this exact project

Remixing the pen project

Remixing is the process of taking another's project and making it your own. For this recipe, we'll pretend that you downloaded (or opened in the Scratch community) the recipe you just created and are about to change it.

Keep in mind, you may have been remixing throughout this book without even knowing! If you, at any point, took a recipe from this book and then changed it around to customize it, you were remixing.

Getting ready

We're going to do some very simple remixing in this recipe. We'll aim to accomplish two things. First, we'll have the sprite return to the center of the stage upon finishing drawing the square. We'll also trigger the drawing of the square with the press of a button.

All you need to do to get started is open up the Scratch file from the previous recipe.

How to do it...

This is what we need to do to get this remix started:

1. On the project page (this is what you see when you find someone else's project in the Scratch community), you would normally click on a button to see inside the project. From there, you have the option to **Remix** the project. From this point forward, we'll assume we've done that part.

2. Head to the script area to add a new sprite to the stage:

3. From the **Things** folder, select **button3** and click on **OK**.

4. Click on the **Costumes** area for the new sprite (the button). Click on **edit** and add the text **Go** to the sprite.

5. Click on **OK**.
6. Your stage will now look something like this:

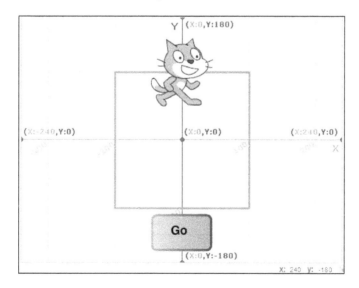

7. Open the script area for the button.
8. Change the name of the sprite in the sprite settings to **Button**.

9. From the **Events** category, drag over a **when this sprite clicked** top hat block.

10. Also, drag over a **broadcast ()** block.

11. Click on the drop-down arrow and create a new message called **drawSquare**.

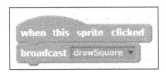

12. Under the **sprite1** script area, replace the original top hat block with a **when I receive ()** block.

13. At the end of the script, drag a **go to x: () y: ()** block and set the values to 0 and 0. The code will then be like this:

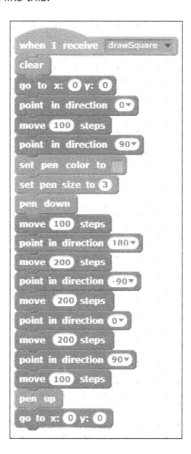

Now you can click on the button. You should see the same result as for the previous recipe, except now the sprite will be repositioned to the center of the stage after completing the square.

Collaboration

In this appendix, we will cover:

- ▸ The online Scratch community
- ▸ Creating an account
- ▸ Sharing projects
- ▸ Sharing scratch 1.4 projects
- ▸ Downloading projects

Introduction

One of the fun things you can do in Scratch is collaborating with other people on your ideas for Scratch, aside from just talking to a person you already know, Scratch is designed to make it easy for you to communicate and share your work with others throughout the world.

This appendix is going to take you through the process of using all of the features out there that will help you to collaborate on Scratch projects, and share your work.

The online Scratch community

When MIT developed Scratch, they wanted you to be able to collaborate. To do this, they created an online community where you can share your projects, view others, and even comment on others. This recipe will serve as an introduction into what that community looks like.

Getting ready

All you have to do to get started is head over to `http://scratch.mit.edu`, the same place you went to download (or use) Scratch to begin with.

How to do it...

Here are the steps to get familiar with the website.

1. Open your browser.
2. Navigate to `http://scratch.mit.edu`.
3. See the upcoming section for more details on what each section of the website has in store for you.

How it works...

Now let's focus on how the website is designed and works. This will make it easy for you to go through the rest of the recipes in this appendix.

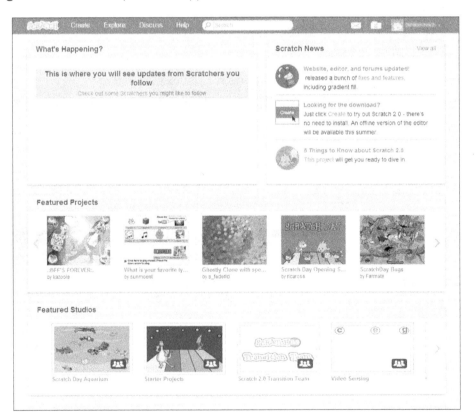

The picture here is what the top of the home page on the Scratch website looks like. Let's break it down by category.

1. **Create**: By now you are probably very familiar with what happens when you click on this button. This is what opens Scratch in your browser so you can get creating. You don't necessarily need to be signed into the website to create, but signing in will allow you to save your work to the Scratch website. When you click on **Create**, a blank Scratch project will open:

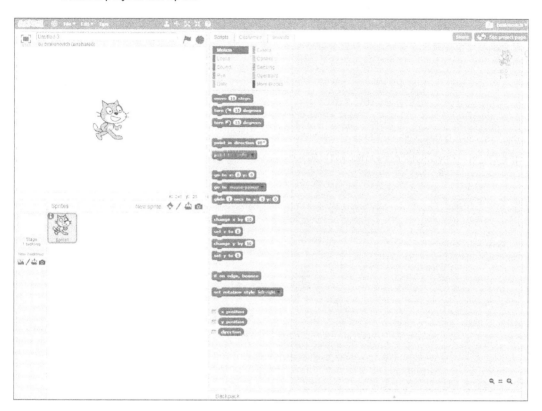

2. **Explore**: The **Explore** area allows us to do just that, explore projects that might interest us. When clicking on that link you'll see several potential categories of projects as well as many projects that match that category.

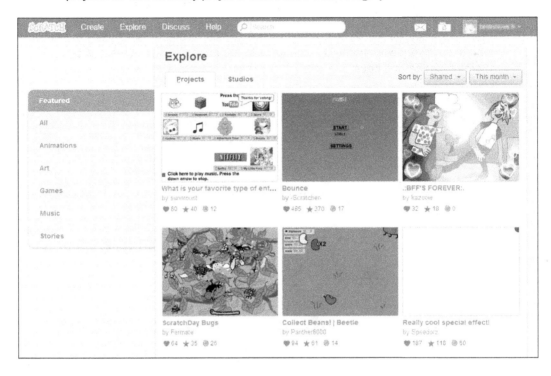

3. **Discuss**: If you're looking to connect and collaborate with other Scratchers, heading to the **Discuss** section is meant for you. You'll see a variety of forums that you can participate in (as long as you are logged in). Post to these forums, or reply to others, whatever it takes to connect with other Scratchers.

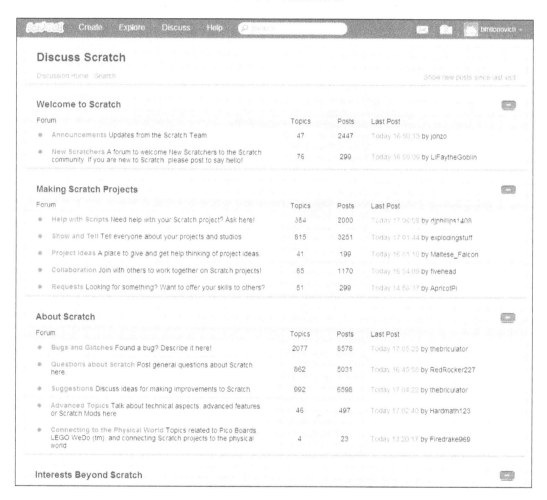

4. **Help**: With Scratch 2.0 the creators added even more help that you can turn to. Use this section if you are stuck on how to do something, and are looking for a resource beyond this book. There are many different guides that can help add to your knowledge base.

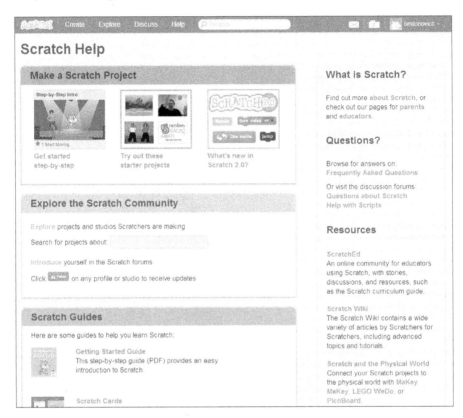

5. **Messages** (applies to being logged in only): You'll see a few more icons in the top-right corner of the page.

The first of these that looks like an envelope brings you to messages that are hanging around for you. You'll see here any comments that have been left on your projects, or any alerts that the creators of Scratch have left you.

6. **My Stuff**: The next button in the upper right brings you to your stuff. You'll see here any projects you uploaded with the older version of Scratch, as well as anything you've created in Scratch 2.0. You can organize your projects into what are called **Studios**, which are similar to folders on your computer.

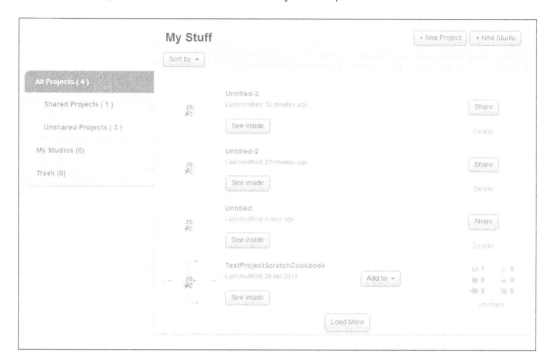

 Looking for something specific in a project? Type into the search bar near the top to search for what you're looking for!

See also

▸ Jump into the next recipe, *Creating an account*, to create your account in Scratch and join the fun!

Creating an account

Creating an account is the first step in really getting involved on the Scratch website.

Getting ready

All you have to do to get started is head over to `http://scratch.mit.edu`, the same place you went to download Scratch to begin with!

How to do it...

Go through the following steps to get your account created on the Scratch website:

1. At the top of the page, click on the **Join Scratch** link, as shown in the following screenshot:

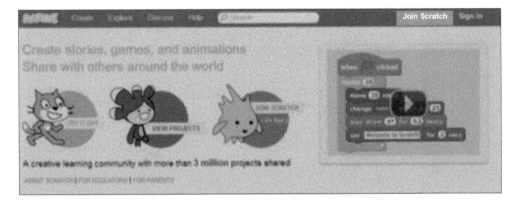

2. You'll be presented with a page that looks something like this:

3. Click on **Next**.

4. Enter a bit of personal information, as shown in the following screenshot:

5. Click on **Next**.

6. You'll see a confirmation page, like the following:

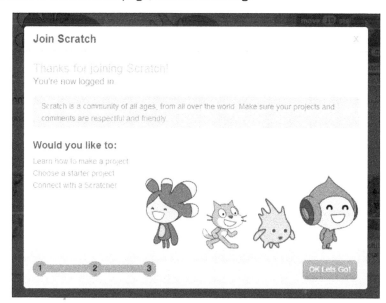

7. That's it; you're ready to get going with all of the features of the website and Scratch!

See also

Learn how to upload projects in the next recipe, *Sharing projects*.

Sharing projects

This recipe is all about sharing projects you've created to the Scratch website.

Getting ready

To prepare for this recipe, create something in Scratch that you want to share with the world.

How to do it...

Perform the following steps to get your project accessible to the world.

1. Open the Scratch file you want to share. We've opened a test file that we'll share.

     Since projects in Scratch 2.0 are created on the Scratch community website itself, there is no true need to upload (unless you are uploading a Scratch 1.4 project). The main change we are making here is making our project public instead of private.

2. You'll see a button at the top of the page on the right side that says **Share**.

3. Your project is now live for folks to see. Click on the button next to the **Share** button to see what your project looks like to the world!

4. The project page is also where you can change the information that the folks see about your project:

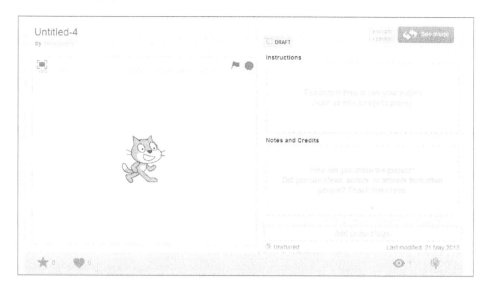

Learn how to download projects in the next recipe, *Sharing Scratch 1.4 projects*.

Sharing Scratch 1.4 projects

If you've been working with Scratch for a while, you were probably using Scratch 1.4. The great news is that with Scratch 2.0 you can upload projects from the older version of Scratch to the newer version of Scratch. This is a nice and easy process.

Getting ready

Create your account on the Scratch website and be sure you are logged in. Open up Scratch.

How to do it...

Follow these steps:

1. Click on the **File** menu.
2. Select the option **Upload from your computer**.
3. Navigate through the folders on your computer to find the file you want to upload to the Scratch community.

4. Your file will upload into Scratch 2.0 and you can save it there as any other Scratch 2.0 file.

Note that once you upload a file to Scratch 2.0 from Scratch 1.4, you can't go in the other direction and bring it back to Scratch 1.4. This is pretty common with most software and programming.

Downloading projects

If you liked *Chapter 9, Project Remixing*, you're probably going to want to download a lot of projects to work with! This is a fun way to get new projects to work on.

Getting ready

Create your account on the Scratch website and be sure that you are logged in. Then head to a project page for a project that you're interested in downloading.

How to do it...

Follow these steps and you'll be ready to remix in no time:

1. On the project page there will be a small box that allows you to **See inside**.

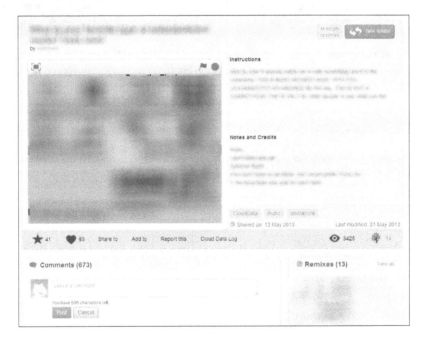

2. You'll see the project as if it were your own. You can change the project and remix it on the downloadable version of Scratch (to be released Summer 2013) or continue with these steps.

 Note that if you want to remix a project, you might just want to hit the remix button that has been added to Scratch 2.0. This will save the project as your own, allowing you to add your own touches to it.

3. Click on **File** and choose **Download to your computer**.

 Note that you don't need to download the project unless you want to work directly on your computer. You can just work on the project in your browser as well. Also, note that if you have Scratch 1.4 installed, anything created in Scratch 2.0 will not open. In other words, Scratch files downloaded will be .sb2 files instead of .sb files. Keep in mind that .sb2 files will not open in Scratch 1.4.

You are now set to use Scratch to collaborate and share with the entire Scratch community (and the world)!

Index

Thank you for buying
Scratch Cookbook

About Packt Publishing

Packt, pronounced 'packed', published its first book "*Mastering phpMyAdmin for Effective MySQL Management*" in April 2004 and subsequently continued to specialize in publishing highly focused books on specific technologies and solutions.

Our books and publications share the experiences of your fellow IT professionals in adapting and customizing today's systems, applications, and frameworks. Our solution based books give you the knowledge and power to customize the software and technologies you're using to get the job done. Packt books are more specific and less general than the IT books you have seen in the past. Our unique business model allows us to bring you more focused information, giving you more of what you need to know, and less of what you don't.

Packt is a modern, yet unique publishing company, which focuses on producing quality, cutting-edge books for communities of developers, administrators, and newbies alike. For more information, please visit our website: www.packtpub.com.

About Packt Open Source

In 2010, Packt launched two new brands, Packt Open Source and Packt Enterprise, in order to continue its focus on specialization. This book is part of the Packt Open Source brand, home to books published on software built around Open Source licences, and offering information to anybody from advanced developers to budding web designers. The Open Source brand also runs Packt's Open Source Royalty Scheme, by which Packt gives a royalty to each Open Source project about whose software a book is sold.

Writing for Packt

We welcome all inquiries from people who are interested in authoring. Book proposals should be sent to author@packtpub.com. If your book idea is still at an early stage and you would like to discuss it first before writing a formal book proposal, contact us; one of our commissioning editors will get in touch with you.

We're not just looking for published authors; if you have strong technical skills but no writing experience, our experienced editors can help you develop a writing career, or simply get some additional reward for your expertise.

open source
community experience distilled

[PACKT]
PUBLISHING

Scratch 1.4

Learn to program while creating interactive
stories, games, and multimedia projects
using Scratch

Beginner's Guide

Michael Badger

Scratch 1.4 Beginner's Guide
Unity 3D Game

ISBN: 978-1-847196-76-7   Paperback: 264 pages

Learn to program while creating interactive stories,
games, and multimedia projects using Scratch

1. Create interactive stories, games, and multimedia
   projects that you can reuse in your own classroom

2. Learn computer programming basics – no
   computer science degree required

3. Connect with the Scratch community for
   inspiration, advice, and collaboration

4. Provides hands-on projects that help you learn by
   experiment and play

Unity 3D Game Development
by Example

A seat-of-your-pants manual for building fun,
groovy little games quickly

Beginner's Guide

Ryan Henson Creighton

Unity 3D Game Development
by Example Beginner's Guide

ISBN: 978-1-849690-54-6   Paperback: 384 pages

A seat-of-your-pants manuel for building fun, groovy little
games quickly

1. Build fun games using the free Unity 3D game
   engine even if you've never coded before

2. Learn how to "skin" projects to make totally
   different games from the same file – more games,
   less effort!

3. Deploy your games to the Internet so that your
   friends and family can play them

4. Packed with ideas, inspiration, and advice for your
   own game design and development

Please check **www.PacktPub.com** for information on our titles

Unity 3.x Game Development by Example Beginner's Guide

ISBN: 978-1-849691-84-0   Paperback: 408 pages

A seat-of-your-pants manual for building fun, groovy little games quickly with Unity 3.x

1. Build fun games using the free Unity game engine even if you've never coded before

2. Learn how to "skin" projects to make totally different games from the same file – more games, less effort!

3. Deploy your games to the Internet so that your friends and family can play them

jQuery Plugin Development Beginner's Guide

ISBN: 978-1-849512-24-4   Paperback: 288 pages

Build powerful, interactive plug-ins to implement jQuery to its best

1. Utilize jQuery's plugin framework to create a wide range of useful jQuery plugins from scratch

2. Understand development patterns and best practices and move up the ladder to master plugin development

3. Discover the ins and outs of some of the most popular jQuery plugins in action

Please check **www.PacktPub.com** for information on our titles

www.ingramcontent.com/pod-product-compliance
Lightning Source LLC
Chambersburg PA
CBHW080400060326
40689CB00019B/4082